MANI AND RUDOLF STEINER

D1028703

MANI
&
RUDOLF STEINER

*Manichaeism, Anthroposophy,
and their Meeting in the Future*

Christine Gruwez

SteinerBooks | 2014

2014

SteinerBooks

An imprint of Anthroposophic Press, Inc.
610 Main St., Great Barrington, MA 01230
www.steinerbooks.org

Cover and book design: William Jens Jensen
Cover image: *Manichaean Electae,* Kocho, Khocho, 10th century;
painting on silk; Museum für Indische Kunst, Berlin

LIBRARY OF CONGRESS CONTROL NUMBER 2014943828

ISBN: 978-1-62148-108-9 (paperback)
ISBN: 978-1-62148-109-6 (eBook)

CONTENTS

Mani and Rudolf Steiner

"*I reveal to you, my child, my loved one: Whoever wills life and to add life to life, long-suffering is what awaits him. Because without long-suffering, he will not be able to live. For long-suffering has everything within it.*"

IAIN GARDNER, "The Reconstruction of Mani's Epistles," article in *The Light and Darkness: Studies in Manichaeism and its World* (Brill 2011)

"*The profound thought that lies in this is that the kingdom of darkness has to be overcome by the kingdom of light, not by means of punishment, but through mildness; not by resisting evil, but by uniting with it in order to redeem evil as such. Because a part of the light enters into evil, the evil itself is overcome.*"

RUDOLF STEINER, *The Temple Legend* (CW 93, November 11, 1904)

INTRODUCTION

The question of the relationship between Anthroposophy and the Manichaean stream immediately evokes the question of the nature of what Rudolf Steiner has achieved by developing Spiritual Science and making it accessible in the course of his life.

The term *Manichaean stream* points both to Manichaeism as it developed from the third century after Christ, and to a future Manichaeism in the way Rudolf Steiner has thrown light on the intention of Manichaeism that points to the future. In this book, both aspects of what can be called the Manichaean stream will be considered: historical Manichaeism and the Mani intention that points to the future.

We are using the term *Spiritual Science* for the whole of Rudolf Steiner's life work—a totality from which, at a certain time, Anthroposophy emerged as its own unique accomplishment. Spiritual Science encompasses the method of research as well as its results, including the various forms and disciplines in which these results were manifested and communicated.

We leave aside the question of to what extent the terms *Spiritual Science* and *Anthroposophy* are interchangeable. In his book on Gnosticism and Anthroposophy, John van Schaik[1] presents elements to distinguish between the two but, at the same time, indicates that it is difficult to be consistent in this distinction. Spiritual Science would then refer more to the dynamic aspect of the path of cognition, while Anthroposophy would rather point to the formal aspect of the content, the knowledge.

But the term *Spiritual Science* alone can cause misunderstandings by creating the impression that it is in the first place about a science and, consequently, a possible transfer of knowledge, albeit knowledge of the deepest grounds of human existence. If that were the only object, to what extent would the insights offered by Steiner's Spiritual Science, no matter how enriching, add something new to the sum of wisdom that has grown through all cultures into a great human treasure? We hope to shed light on this question by showing certain connections between the Manichaean stream and Spiritual Science.

When Spiritual Science can be understood as a path of research the question gets a different character. Seen from this angle, a natural distinction arises between research as a method and the research results. However, this distinction cannot prevent the potential of the research results being separated from the research as such, thus becoming a kind of autonomous body of knowledge, in other words, of things that can be learned and known.

ANTHROPOSOPHY AS DEED?

"I have to do it, but it is not about me!"

Perhaps the really new aspect of Anthroposophy could be that, besides an indispensable insight, it also encompasses an equally indispensable deed. A justifiable objection could here be that, for instance, Steiner's philosophy of freedom, Christology, or threefold social order are absolutely new ideas within the realm of anthroposophic thinking. Nevertheless, one could say that as long as these new insights are not transformed into deeds, nothing has changed.

What is here called a deed is not the same as putting insights that can grow out of research results into practice, although of course this does not in the least diminish the incontestable value of the practical work that has come out of Anthroposophy in society. On the contrary! It does mean, however, that within a field of activity it is possible, side by side with the practical realization of insights, to come to a deed. What is meant with a deed in this context can only be elucidated in the perspective of the Mani intention.

Neither can what is here called a deed coincide with working on oneself in the sense of developing the spiritual element in oneself through concentration and meditation, no matter how meaningful, even necessary, this may be. The path of schooling is itself, first of all, a field of activity, for although it might be limited to acquiring knowledge of various insights, it is also possible, in the course of the path of schooling, to fulfill this work on oneself by deeds in the Manichaean sense.

Anthroposophy as deed does not appear in its full reality until it is viewed in the light of Manichaeism or, rather, against the light and darkness that in Manichaeism initiates, as creative primal principles, the development of the human being and the cosmos.

The scarce and seemingly reluctant statements by Rudolf Steiner in this connection point in the direction of a realization that, once we have become aware of it, can no longer be avoided. And it is the great merit of Bernard Lievegoed that he gave the stream of Manichaeism its justified place in the context of what is moving in Anthroposophy as an all-encompassing stream in humanity. After all, the salvation of the soul,[2] the central motif of Manichaeism, is a deed, a deed to which we are called as people of our time. Knowledge and wisdom may indeed help us, but they can be no substitutes for the actual deed. It is a deed we must perform but does not relate to us. In the words of Bernard Lievegoed:

> More and more people will find methods to help others in the most surprising ways. To put yourself in the service of the difficulties of another person, that is the point.[3]

After a historical introduction in chapter 1, we will shed light in chapter 2 on some particular questions regarding Mani's teaching. We will also consider there the question of the nature of Mani's dualism as well as the question of his individuality. We will look at these questions in the light of the point of view and statements of Rudolf Steiner. Chapter 3 is wholly devoted to the Mani intention, the future mission of Manichaeism and how this can already be prepared in our time. Rudolf Steiner's insights regarding the role of good and evil in the creation and in human beings are of decisive significance in this discussion. Finally, we will focus in chapter 4 on the unique character of Mani's individuality from the viewpoint of his artistry and the significance of art in the whole of his life and message. Here we can also find an indication of the intention of Manichaeism in the future.

MANI AND MANICHAEISM: THE HISTORICAL DIMENSION

A thousand books will be preserved...; they will come into the hands of the just and the faithful...the Gospel and the Treasury of Life, the Pragmateia and the Book of Mysteries, the Book of Giants and the Epistles, the Psalms and the Prayers of [my] Lord, the Icon [Picture Book] and his Revelations, his Parables and his Mysteries.... How many will be lost? How many will be destroyed? A thousand lost, another thousand recovered, for they will find them at the end. They will kiss them and say: "O Wisdom of Greatness, O Armor of the Apostle! When you were lost..., where did they find you?" And you shall find them reading them aloud, uttering the name [of each book] among them, the name of its lord; and the name of those who gave all [for it to be written] and the name of the scribe who wrote it and of the one who punctuated it...[4]

Manichaeism Rediscovered

When the above prediction was written, the author will not have foreseen that some 1700 years later the wisdom books of Mani, the Apostle of Light, would come into the hands of archeologists and scholars who, each out of their own discipline, would bring Manichaeism to light again. Indeed, since the beginning of the twentieth century, a number of spectacular discoveries has focused much attention on Manichaeism in an entirely new way.

Until that time, texts of Mani's antagonists and descriptions by Persian and Arabic historians in more general books about the history of their countries were the only sources of information about Manichaeism. Since both of these categories of source material contain direct quotations from Manichaean scriptures, Isaac de Bausobre was able to publish a first comprehensive, non-polemical document on Manichaeism already in the eighteenth century.[5]

The new discoveries began with a series of archeological expeditions between 1902 and 1914 to the edge of the Taklamakan desert in today's autonomous region of Xinjiang in western China. They became known as the Royal Prussian Turfan Expeditions. They found authentic Manichaean documents in several languages, fragments of miniatures, paintings on silk, and frescoes. Countless caves along the Silk Road turned out to be not merely cultic and meditation places for Buddhist and Nestorian travelers, but they also showed traces of the cult, practices, and customs as these were living in Manichaean communities. This is confirmed by the unmistakably Manichaean wall paintings in several meditation caves, mostly in the area of the Turfan Oasis, such as those in Bezeklik and Toyuq. There are also ruins of monasteries that are demonstrably Manichaean.

Most of these findings are now preserved in the Museum for Indian Art in Berlin. Their origin can be attributed partly to the presence of Manichaean merchants (most of all the Sogdians; many documents were written in Sogdian, an Iranian language) along the caravan roads in this area. Partly, however, these discoveries are also very closely connected with the history of the Uighur people. Following the conversion of their ruler Boghu Khan in 765, they became Manichaeans. After the invasions of the Kyrgyz people in 840, they pulled back from the Mongolian steppes and moved along the northern branch of the Silk Road to the region of the Turfan Oasis where they settled and established a capital, Kocho, until the middle of the thirteenth century. In this same period, Manichaeism also developed influence at the Chinese Imperial court through ambassadors of the Uighur king.

In 731 already a treatise was drawn up by order of the Chinese Emperor describing the essential elements of the Manichaean doctrine, the so-called *Compendium*.[6] As a teaching document it is unique, if only because of the fact that it was preserved in its entirety. Unfortunately, after its discovery in Dun Huang it was divided between Paris and London, because the first four chapters were purchased by Sir Aurel Stein and the remaining two by the French sinologist Pelliot. Quite soon after the discovery the *Journal Asiatique* published a partial translation by Pelliot and Chavannes in 1913.[7]

Further Discoveries

In 1957 a Manichaean temple was discovered on the Huabiao Hill near Quanzhou on the South Chinese coast, which was called Zayton by Marco Polo who met Manichaeans in China when he traveled there in 1292. In addition, since 2000 an Australian team has been working on findings and information recently collected by Chinese archeologists and academics.

A discovery of Manichaean documents from one of the numerous Manichaean communities in North Egypt, followed by their publication in subsequent years, signified a turning point in the rediscovery of Manichaeism. By chance, in 1907 some local workers dug up seven papyrus codices quite intact in their wooden chest. However, it took until 1930 before these precious documents of inestimable value, all of them written in Coptic, came to the attention of the German coptologist Carl Schmidt who, on behalf of the Prussian Academy, wanted to purchase manuscripts in Palestine and to whom, while he was in transit in Cairo, these scrolls were offered.

A year earlier, in 1929, the Danish Egyptologist H. O. Lange had discovered Coptic-Manichaean manuscripts in the area of Medinet Madi. However, the collection of codices had already been split up. Four of them, including the *Kephalaia of the Teacher* went to Berlin while the remaining three, including the *Homilies* and the *Psalms*, were later acquired by the Irish-American businessperson Chester Beatty. Since World War II these latter have been preserved in the wonderful Chester Beatty Library in Dublin.

In 1933 Schmidt and his colleagues published the first results of their research.[8] From that time the scientific exploration of Manichaeism really gained momentum. In several other places in Egypt documents were found that indicated the existence of Manichaean communities in the region. The most important one among these is ancient Kellis (now named Ismant el-Kharab) in the Dalekh Oasis, where exploration and research is ongoing.

As a result of the discovery in 1969 of the *Cologne Mani Codex* (CMC), the figure of Mani has become known to a wider audience. In 1970 Albert Heinrichs and Ludwig Koenen published the first results of their study of this codex, which was written in Greek with the title *On the Origin of His Body*.[9] Both the form and the content of the codex created great excitement.

The Cologne Mani Codex is one of the smallest codices written on parchment in late antiquity; it measures 1½ by 1¾ inches and has an average of twenty-three lines per page on a total of almost 200 pages! Nowhere is any letter higher than one millimeter (1/25 inch) and, nevertheless, the writing—from the hands of a number of different scribes— is of astonishing beauty and precision. The spaces between words and sentences are always in proportion, and the use of thicker and thinner lines demonstrates all characteristics of artistic calligraphy.

The content is composed as an anthology in which, at one time, Mani himself is speaking; at another, his closest disciples and immediate successors speak. The various episodes that describe events between Mani's fourth and twenty-fourth year follow each other as images of a life that, from its very beginning, prefigured the mission that is connected with him.

On the one hand we learn from this biography that Mani was in constant contact with his *syzygos*, his "twin soul" or higher self, which made revelations to him around his twelfth year and again around his twenty-fourth year. On the other hand, countless moving and sometimes almost miraculous events demonstrate how Mani, even as a child, came into conflict with the laws and rules of the community in which he grew up, and how he finally had to leave the sect, which had been founded by Elchasai. The story tells how he began his life as an itinerant preacher, but then it breaks off.

The Cologne Mani Codex has added important elements to what was known about Mani and his religion until then. It became clear that the Jewish-Christian element is of central importance in Manichaeism, even though Mani opposed certain aspects of it. His outspoken dualism may well have been a reaction to the strict monotheism of the Baptist community of Elchasai.

MANI, THE APOSTLE OF JESUS CHRIST

Mani was born in the year 216 in "al-Madain," the twin city of Seleucia-Ctesiphon, capital and winter residence of the Parthian and later the Sassanid kings of the Persian Empire. In most documents the name of his father, Pattikios, is mentioned, but that of his mother, Maryam, appears only in Arabic and Chinese sources.

When Mani was four years old Pattikios took him away from his mother and brought him to a Jewish-Christian Baptist community where he had already lived for a number of years. This community, one of many in the region, was founded by Elchasai. Mani lived here for twenty years and, as related by the CMC, experienced a profound spiritual development including an initiation by his *syzygos* into the secrets of the creation of the cosmos and the human being. Part of his initiation was the assignment to proclaim the substance of the revelation as a universal message to the world.

After Mani had repeatedly, but fruitlessly, tried to share the truth revealed to him with members of the Elchasaite community, he left the community in the company of a few faithful followers and, later, of his father Pattikios. This moment can be considered as the actual beginning of Mani's preaching and the founding of his religion. This is emphasized by the fact that, when Mani began his twenty-fifth year of life, his *syzygos* explicitly called on him to do this.

From then on, Mani traveled around preaching on the Iranian plateau and through the extended provinces of the Persian Empire. He called himself a physician (that is, a healer), a "messiah," who came from the land of Babylon (at that time a province of the Persian Empire) and performed miraculous healings. He is also said to have journeyed through the Persian Gulf to India, where he spread his teaching further.

After King Ardashir's death in 241, he returned to Iran and was present at the crowning of Shapur I, Ardashir's successor, a ruler who wanted to expand and strengthen the Sassanid dynasty. Mani was then introduced to the king by Peroz, governor of Merv and brother of Shapur. Mani's appearance and bearing made a deep impression on Shapur who then permitted him to preach within the borders of his realm. In those years Mani established the center of his community in Seleucia-Ctesiphon from where his followers always went out to carry his message to East and West.

After the death of Shapur in 273, Mani was able to continue his activities without interference under Hormizd I, but Hormizd died within a year and was succeeded in 274 by Vahram I. From the beginning of his reign, Vahram stood under the influence of the powerful Zoroastrian priests and considered Mani as someone who threatened the unity of the Empire. In order to reinforce this unity, Kartir, the high priest, proclaimed the Zoroastrian cult as the one and only religion of the Persian Empire. All other religions were then persecuted and the Manichaean communities in particular suffered from this eradication policy. In the end, Mani was summoned to Gondishapur, the city that was founded by Shapur as a center for science and culture. The decisive conversation between Vahram I and Mani, the arguments for his death sentence and a description of the last days of his life, which he spent surrounded by disciples and followers, have been preserved in Coptic texts.

Mani died a martyr's death in 276. In Coptic documents, particularly in the *Homilies*, we find an extensive description of the last interview between Vahram I and Mani, and also of Mani's suffering and death. In this last interview, which seems more like an interrogation, the king asked for Mani's justification of his actions and preaching in the realm. Mani emphasized that he had neither master nor teacher, but acted entirely on his own. The mission to travel around and spread his message had been given to him by means of his *syzygos*, his higher self, and therefore came directly from the Father of Greatness himself. It was the Truth that was revealed to him, Mani.

The king's reply speaks volumes: "Why did God reveal this Truth to Mani and not to me, who am King of these lands?" Mani's answer is only partly preserved, but was the only one possible: "All power is in the hands of God"—implying therefore, not in the hands of worldly rulers.

These words, the last that Mani spoke in public—during the 26 days of his suffering he still had many conversations with his disciples—set the tone, as it were. The motive for the persistent persecution and eradication with which Manichaeism was to be fought, both in the West and in the East, lies in this answer by Mani to the king's question, like the germ in a seed. The Manichaeans acknowledge but one source of legitimate power, namely that of the divine Father of Light himself. And this is the one—and no other—who gives them the power to act as individuals in the world.

MANI'S SCRIPTURES

The canonical scriptures from the hand of Mani himself are known from various sources. In most cases it is a list of seven titles, sometimes nine. In several texts we find statements by Mani in which he explicitly set the religion he proclaimed above the pronouncements of the other religions. He justified this by the fact that, unlike for instance Buddha and Jesus, he himself wrote down the content of his teaching.

The large majority of these canonical works has been lost. But we still possess a fairly complete overview of their content because of the work of Arabic historians and reviewers such as al-Biruni (973–1048) and Ibn al-Nadim (died 995 or 998). Sometimes we also have fragments and quotations in other Manichaean texts, such as the *Living Gospel* in the CMC, parallel texts in Sogdian or Parthian (e.g., the *Book of Giants*), as well as quotations in the works of Church Fathers and opponents.

The scriptures described below were all written in an eastern variant of Aramaic, sometimes called Syriac, a language that was spoken as a kind of *lingua franca* in the Near and Middle East, and that Mani undoubtedly knew. The *Shabuhragan*, however, the first work that Mani wrote for the Persian King Shapur I, was written in Middle Persian.

1. The Living Gospel

The Living Gospel has 22 chapters, labeled according to the letters of the Aramaic alphabet. In the Coptic tradition, it is called "the king" of Mani's scriptures, and without doubt it deserves first place among Mani's canonical scriptures. According to al-Biruni (in his book *al-Athar*) it is in this book that Mani proclaimed himself to be the Paraclete announced by Jesus. This work undoubtedly had the function of gospel and catechism in one. The Manichaean missionaries took it with them for their missions. Since for this reason it was translated into many languages it is not surprising that the CMC contains three quotations from this gospel in Greek.

2. The Treasury of Life

This is a systematic treatise on the content of Mani's teaching, probably for the purpose of justifying the Manichaean community. Excerpts can be found, among others, in St. Augustine's works (i.e., in *De natura boni*, 44, and *Contra Felicem*, II-5) and in al-Biruni who quoted some statements. In this scripture Mani is said to have spoken of the "Third Missionary." In the *Kephalaia* it is mentioned that Mani wrote in this book about "The Good Pearl."

3. The Book of Mysteries

Almost nothing was preserved of this book, but the *Fihrist* by Ibn al-Nadim, the "Catalog" that he completed in Baghdad in 988, contains a detailed table of contents of this scripture. For instance, in chapter IV there is mention of the "Son of the Widow." According to Ibn al-Nadim this refers to Jesus, the Messiah who was crucified by the Jews and was the son of the widow Mary. From the table of contents it appears that in this work it was Mani's principal purpose to make a stand in a number of controversies concerning his teaching, such as questions as to his position as a prophet, the end of time, and the last judgment. He referred to a number of apocryphal texts for this, including some of Christian origin. In the fifth chapter Mani relates a number of pronouncements by Jesus and, according to Ibn al-Nadim, the tenth chapter was about Adam's testimony of Jesus.

4. Pragmateia, or Legends

This is a collection of legends of a cosmological nature. It is assumed that Mani collected the legends in order to respond to questions of his followers as to how the creation occurred. In spite of the heterogeneous nature of this work, it presents a consistent story from the attack of the Realm of Darkness on the Realm of Light until the time when the first human being was awakened on Earth by Jesus the Splendor. This work with its often bizarre pictures was later the source of countless quotations by opponents of Manichaeism, for the obvious reason that its content easily invited mockery. Some parts of the eleventh *Book of Scholia* by the Nestorian bishop and opponent Theodore bar Konai, who lived in the eighth century in Babylonia, are based on this work of Mani.

5. The Book of Giants

The Book of Giants was written for the Parthian speaking tribes in the Persian Empire. The *Kephalaia*, in the list of Mani's works, contains the following quotation of Mani: "I have written this work at the request of the Parthians." This is also a book of wonderful cosmic imaginations in which the central theme is the battle against gigantic monsters and dragons until in the end the heroes, in this case two brothers, gain the victory in this battle against giants. Sources of inspiration for this scripture could be Jewish apocalyptic writings, in particular the apocalypse of Enoch.

6. Epistles

These are missionary letters in the style of the letters of St. Paul. According to Ibn al-Nadim it appears that Mani wrote a large number of letters; he was probably the most productive letter writer in the Sassanid Empire of his time. Some letters contain teaching, they give advice in regard to fasting, the celebration of festivals, or they respond to practical life questions and stimulate communities that are losing momentum. The letters have headings such as "Letter on the two principles," "Missionary letter to Armenia," "Letter on paradise." In al-Nadim's list 76 letters are shown. This separate codex with letters by Mani was brought to Berlin by Carl Schmidt together with the other codices. Unfortunately, at the end of World War II this codex had disappeared together with other priceless documents, probably looted by Soviet troops or else destroyed in the bombings.

7. Psalms and Prayers

From Coptic tradition it is known that Mani wrote psalms and prayers, but these do not form part of the Coptic Book of Psalms of Medinet Madi, although the latter does mention prayers and two psalms that Mani was reported to have composed.

8. Picture Book

This book has the Middle Persian title of *Ardahang* while in the Coptic tradition it is called *Eikon*. In the Chinese *Compendium* it is called *Picture* at the end of the listing of Mani's canonical scriptures; there it is also called *Picture of the Two Great Principles*. It is a book consisting of illustrations made by Mani himself in which he attempts to unfold a comprehensive imagery of his cosmogony by means of a consistent series of successive pictures. Some texts explain that it is a visual presentation of the *Living Gospel*. The *Picture Book* was immensely famous, also outside the circle of Manichaeans, and led to the fact that even today Mani is considered in Iran as the founder of the Persian art of miniature painting.

9. Shabuhragan

The *Shabuhragan* is a teaching document written in Middle Persian at the request of King Shapur I, with whom Mani had a good relationship, and who protected him. It is possible to reconstruct a large part of this work from the fragments found in the Turfan Oasis. The fragments contain a part of the creation story and an eschatological part that has to do with the events at the end of time. This work is also important because it was the first one that he wrote, at the beginning of his public activity.

The Organization of a Manichaean Community

In the first place, the Manichaeans made a distinction among each other between *Electi* (literally the chosen ones) and *Auditores* (listeners or students); these are the Latin terms used by, among others, St. Augustine and other Christian authors. In the Iranian world, they were called *Ardavan* (qualified ones) and *Nyoshagan* (listeners). The *Electi* were the ones who had made the vow strictly to follow the rules of the Manichaean way of life. They strove for truthfulness, love, patience, faith, and joy; they lived in blissful poverty, did not have a profession, and made sure that they did nothing that might harm a human being, animal, or plant. In addition, they fasted weekly on Sunday and Monday besides the greater fasts in preparation for festivals. They practiced daily prayer and meditation, did not marry, and abstained from meat and fermented drink. Their tasks included devoting themselves entirely to spreading the message of Mani and to organizing the great festivals and confession meetings.

However, the *Electi* did not live in isolation. Many of them lived as itinerant preachers and traveled great distances during which they came in contact with the most diverse cultures and religions. Also within a Manichaean community there was no separation between *Electi* and *Auditores*. Meetings and liturgical festivals took place in the presence of the entire community. What made them different was their way of life and the rules they had to observe. The *Auditores* also fasted, mainly on Sundays, and took part in the public confession meetings on Mondays. The purpose of the guidelines that governed their way of life, sometimes called the Ten Commandments, was to help them walk the path of the right teaching. For instance, worshipping idols, engaging in magic, practicing polygamy, stealing, and deceiving were forbidden. But the rule against harming human beings, animals, or plants also applied to them. Avarice had to be transformed into generosity, and innocent people had to be given assistance.

This dual nature of every Manichaean community was subdivided into five levels of which the bottom one was formed by the *Auditores*. Immediately above them stood a large group of *Electi*, which included the scribes, cantors, missionaries, and choirmasters. Women and men could be part of these categories and there was no limit on their numbers. Three higher levels formed, as it were, the spiritual center of the community and limits did exist on their numbers. There were 360 *presbyters* on the third level, seventy-two bishops on the fourth, and twelve teachers on the fifth and highest level. Perhaps surprisingly, these levels did not in reality form a pyramidal structure; we should rather think of five concentric circles, especially because in the center of the circle of twelve there was a thirteenth, the *archegos*, who formed the spiritual center of the community.

Liturgy and Prayer

Life in a Manichaean community had a rhythm for those who had made the vow, the *Electi*, as well as for the laity, the *Auditores*, because of the daily prayers—four times a day for the *Auditores* and seven times for the *Electi*. During the day people faced the sun during their prayers, at night the moon. A ritual meal took place every day at which the *Electi* took in the food in such a way that, as a result of their inner purity, they were able to absorb the light from it. The laity could be present at this meal (they were the ones who brought the fruits and vegetables) but did not participate in it.

Then there was the weekly public confession conversation on Mondays about which we have information in a text with the title *Chinese Confession Mirror*. Fasts and wakes (during which hymns and psalms were sung) were fixed throughout the year as preparations for feast days, and culminated in a thirty-day fast that prepared for the Bema festival. This fast was concluded by an annual great confession meeting. *Bema* means "platform" or "dais," and in the Manichaean cult the platform had five steps, symbolizing the fivefold structure of the community. The highest level, however, remained unoccupied. It was reserved for Mani, whose invisible yet real presence formed the center of the community.

The Bema festival was the high point of the liturgical year, because it celebrated Mani's dying and therefore his liberation. The night before the celebration, which also concluded the thirty-day fast, was passed in prayer and singing hymns by the whole community. At dawn the doors of the hall were opened so that the first sunlight could stream in and illuminate the place where the throne of Mani was erected. The celebration was one of overwhelming joy. It was not just a memorial of Mani's martyr's death, but he was present in all reality and acted as a sign of hope for the future liberation of all light.

The Message of Mani

None of the documents that have come to light so far, with the exception of the extremely concise Chinese *Compendium*,[10] contain a complete description of Mani's teaching, encompassing his cosmogony (the creation story), anthropology (the role of the human being in the creation), and eschatology (the creation of a new world order). However, it is part of the unique character of Mani's teaching that these three elements are like inherent parts of one organism. They form an indivisible whole.

If we may characterize Mani's system as a teaching of the salvation of the world, then the cosmogony describes how a desperate situation developed, his anthropology answers the question of how and by whom this situation can be resolved, so that finally the description of the end of time can indicate the outcome that can be expected that will save the world. The basic structure of this organic unity of the teaching can be recognized in the compact formula used in Chinese treatises to describe Mani's message: "the doctrine of two principles and three epochs."

The two principles are light and darkness. The three epochs are:

- Non-interference between light and dark
- Interference between both principles and the mingling of light and darkness
- Separation between light and darkness.

We can read extensive descriptions of Mani's cosmogony in a number of publications.[11] Here we will limit ourselves to a summary followed by a discussion of several principal questions regarding Mani's teaching in the light of Rudolf Steiner's approach to Manichaeism. It should be noted that in our summary of Mani's teaching we are basing ourselves primarily on Iranian source material and the imagery it contains. The intervention of Jesus the Splendor is an episode derived from Theodore bar Konai.

The Creation Story

First Epoch: Since all eternity two kingdoms have been in existence side by side: the Kingdom of Light and the Kingdom of Darkness. Both are uncreated and eternal. The Kingdom of Light borders to the south on the Kingdom of Darkness.

Second Epoch, the Mingling: A crisis develops when the powers of Darkness, the *archontes*, catch a glimpse of the Light and wish to conquer the Kingdom of Light. The Kingdom of Light decides to go and meet the Darkness. This takes place in three successive phases of creation.

- *First creation:* The Father of Greatness, the King of the Light, brings forth out of himself the Mother of Life, and from these two emanates the as yet uncreated first human being. The first human being girds himself with the five light elements—ether, light, wind, water, and fire—and enters the Darkness. The *archontes*, the beings in the Kingdom of Darkness, overwhelm him and tear apart his living light soul, the five elements. Light is now mixed with Darkness.

- *Second creation:* Three representatives of the Light now engage the powers of Darkness in battle, with the result that the creation begins. From the mixed substance, meaning the *archontes* who have devoured the light, are born ten heavens, eight earths, the heavenly bodies, and the elements of wind, fire, and water.

- *Third creation:* Again, three representatives are sent out by the Light world, now to make preparations for a process of redemption that will lead to the creation of a New Paradise and a New World. On their part, the *archontes* continue to mingle for the purpose of creating human beings who will be completely in their power. The first representative sent by the Father of Light is accompanied by twelve light maidens after whose image the *archontes* form the first human being on Earth. Jesus the Splendor comes to this human being and awakens him to self-knowledge, which enables him to become a participant in the redemption process.

Third Epoch: After successive periods of devastation and after the war of all against all, followed by the great fire, Jesus—in Iranian tradition also called Mihr Yazd—will appear as judge and, in an all-encompassing purification process, separate the just from those who obstinately continue to adhere to evil. The New Earth and New Paradise will then rise up—in Iranian tradition these are called *Frashegird*—and the final remnant of evil will be eternally imprisoned in the center of the Earth.

The Figure of Jesus

In the Manichaean cosmogony, Jesus appears as a three-fold being:

1. Jesus the Splendor who awakens Adam and summons him to participate in the redemption,
2. Jesus Patibilis, the pure Light Soul, who has sacrificed himself in the darkness and is held captive in the creation, "crucified" in matter, and
3. Jesus the Prophet and Messiah. Here Mani considers Jesus as one of the Light Apostles who preceded him.

In the fragments of Mani's *Living Gospel* that form part of the Cologne Mani Codex, Mani calls himself one who was sent, an apostle of Jesus Christ.

2

RUDOLF STEINER AND MANICHAEISM

RUDOLF STEINER'S APPROACH TO MANICHAEISM

In all respects, Rudolf Steiner spoke with a certain modesty and reluctance when Mani and Manichaeism were discussed. It seems as if there was something that held him back from discussing the subject in all its dimensions and in its final consequences ("the ultimate objectives"):

> Unfortunately it is not yet permissible today to unveil the ultimate secrets of this doctrine, even in our present circle...

And in the same lecture:

> I have already said that the time has not yet come to reveal the ultimate secrets of Manichaeism, but it is possible to give a few indications.[12]

In his very first lecture on the subject of Manichaeism, where he also used the words "the Mani intention," Rudolf Steiner indicates that in the future Manichaeism will "make its appearance in many forms. It appears in forms that many can call to mind but that need not be mentioned today."[13]

This does not alter the fact that some of his approaches are nevertheless communicated with great emphasis, for instance when he distances himself from what was often being written about Manichaeism in his time.

One such order was the Manichaean, of which ordinary scholarship gives a quite false picture.... The Manichaeans are supposed to have taught that a Good and an Evil are part of the natural order and have always been in conflict with each other, this having been determined for them by the Creation. Here is a glimmer of the order's real task but distorted to the point of nonsense.[14]

It is clear that what Steiner was referring to here has to do with all that is connected with the future intention of Manichaeism, a task that he then called an extremely difficult one. Also in the lecture of June 25 1908, Steiner mentioned a wide-spread misunderstanding, "merely phrases," when the teaching of Manichaeism was discussed. Immediately thereafter he spoke about "this teaching and its development in the future," indicating that he was again referring to the future intention of Manichaeism.[15] We may conclude from this that the teaching as it has become part of Manichaeism in its historical form needs to be transformed. When Steiner then spoke again about historical Manichaeism, we read the following:

The essence of Manichaean teaching relates to the doctrine of good and evil. In ordinary thought, good and evil are two irreducible qualities, one of which, goodness, must destroy the other, evil. To Manichaeans, however, evil is integral to the cosmos and collaborates in its evolution, and it will eventually be absorbed and transfigured by goodness.[16]

The first time Rudolf Steiner spoke about Manichaeism was on November 11, 1904, in a series of lectures he gave for members of the Theosophical Society in Berlin.[17] And it is also the only time that he dedicated an entire lecture to this subject. Irrespective of what may have been his reasons, it is a fact that in the first few years of the twentieth century the first discoveries were made relating to Manichaeism. In August 1902, the first German expedition under Albert Grünwedel, organized by the Museum für Völkerkunde in Berlin, had departed for the Turfan Oasis where, immediately upon arrival in Kucha, the capital of the Uighur people, they made important discoveries. A second expedition led by Albert von Le Coq, now financed from private means supplied in part by Emperor Wilhelm II, arrived in Kucha in November 1904. Again, in Kucha and its immediate surroundings frescoes, manuscripts, and fragments of miniatures were found. In the same year of 1904, F. W. K. Mueller succeeded in deciphering the, until then, still unknown Manichaean script, which had been created by Mani himself. This made possible the very first translation of original Manichaean scriptures into a European language. Two additional expeditions were to follow.

More than once Rudolf Steiner called attention to the fact that there were many misunderstandings and erroneous interpretations in circulation regarding Manichaeism. He emphatically distanced himself from these a number of times. Actually, in a lecture on May 22, 1920, he made the suggestion not to be too narrowly focused on the literal content of the scriptures, but to develop a feeling for the overall character of this worldview.

> To define this Manichaeism we must say this: There is more importance in the general attitude of this view of life than in what one can literally describe as its contents.[18]

It is interesting that in a number of lectures when Manichaeism was being discussed, St. Augustine also came into view. Of course this is because the great Church Father was an *auditor* for nine years and was thus a member of a Manichaean community. Subsequently, he became the strongest opponent in the West of this same Manichaeism. Steiner then spoke about the change St. Augustine brought in human thinking and, therefore, also in western spiritual life, by making the step from a way of thinking that was filled with images and spirit (as in Manichaeism) to the abstract, self-conscious thinking that would become characteristic of western culture. By this change that, of course, also took place in himself, St. Augustine was no longer able to identify with Manichaeism, said Steiner.

There are four lectures in which Rudolf Steiner spoke about St. Augustine in relation to Manichaeism. These are the following:

> November 11, 1904, in *The Temple Legend*, CW 93,
> May 22, 1920, in *The Philosophy of Thomas Aquinas*, CW 74,
> May 15, 1921, in *Die Naturwissenschaft und die weltgeschichtliche Entwickelung der Menschheit seit dem Altertum*, CW 325, and
> April 29, 1923, in *Die menschliche Seele in ihrem Zusammenhang mit göttlich-geistigen Individualitäten*, CW 224.

St. Augustine did not wait for his conversion to Christianity before he made a thorough study of the teaching of the Manichaean system. A number of passages in the *Confessions*, for instance, clearly indicate that he was quite familiar with Manichaean doctrine. "Thus we may feel certain that, at a young age already and with enthusiasm, St. Augustine studied Manichaeism and its scriptures as an *auditor*."[19] By his participation in Manichaeism over many years, St. Augustine was not only very familiar with its scriptures, but he also realized that the religious system of Mani is completely dependent on the doctrine of the two natures. In his consistent fight against Manichaean teaching, St. Augustine time and again directed his attacks to this point, with which he also wanted to undermine its other doctrines. François Decret, whose research was oriented primarily toward Manichaeism in the context of its spread through North Africa and in relation to St. Augustine, formulated it as follows:

The dogma of the Two Principles is without a doubt the foundation, for without this dogma, the entire religious structure, as Mani had worked it out, collapses. This is precisely what the former *auditor*, St. Augustine, wanted to emphasize when, in order to demonstrate the connection between the dogma of the Two Principles and the teaching of the Two Souls, he wrote that they should stop contending and preaching that there are two souls... and that, if they do this, they should stop being Manichaeans any longer...[20]

In St. Augustine's *Acts against Fortunatus the Manichaean* the debate focused on the dogma of the two principles, during which Fortunatus gave the two principles differing names. St. Augustine's most extensive anti-Manichaean document, *Contra Faustum*, contains the famous passage in which St. Augustine countered the Manichaean doctrine of the two natures by saying that it is in effect a doctrine of "two gods." Obviously he then denounced it as an error. At the end of the debate it remains undecided whether the Manichaean doctrine is one of two natures or two gods (*c. Faustum*, XXI, I).

In *On the Morals of the Manichaeans*, St. Augustine himself spoke about the teaching of the two natures as follows: "If then there are two natures, as you contend, namely the realm of the darkness and the realm of the light, yet you say that the realm of the light is God" (*De moribus*, I, III, 5). He does the same in *On Heresies*, in which "we can find St. Augustine's most complete and organized summary of the Manichaean system."[21] There St. Augustine characterized the two principles as "different from each other and opposed to each other, simultaneously eternal, and in all eternity equal to each other, thus it has always been" while subsequently labeling them as "two natures and substances, namely of good and of evil" (*De Haer*, XLVI, 2).

In some lectures, Rudolf Steiner placed Manichaeism in the foreground when he discussed the views of Christ and Jesus in Gnostic conceptions in the days of early Christianity.

Sometimes he refers also to the theology of his time.[22] Such passages occur especially in the lectures of August 31, 1913, in *The East in the Light of the West* (CW 113), and December 25, 1918, in *How Do I Find Christ?* (CW 187).

Although Steiner was not always fully consistent in the way he spoke about the relationship of Manichaeism to Christ and to Jesus, he did view Manichaeism as a source for later developments of esoteric Christianity. In his words: "Christian esotericism is derived from the Manichaeans..."[23] In another lecture, Steiner described that it was not possible for Mani with his still clairvoyant consciousness to fathom how Christ adopted an earthly form in Jesus. "In Manichaeism we see the struggle to understand the Mystery of Golgotha." And a little further: "That is why they struggled...with the riddle of evil."[24] From the context of the lecture, in which the Mithras cult was also extensively discussed, it is clear that Steiner spoke in this regard of the historical Manichaeism. But in the Christmas lecture on December 25, 1918, we hear: "We still see it [the ancient Gnostic thought force] in Mani in the third century... a great, forceful, grandiose interpretation of the Mystery of Golgotha."[25]

A year earlier, in a lecture in which the figure of Julian the Apostate was extensively discussed, Steiner mentioned Manichaeism as the teaching that "claimed to understand Christ Jesus better than Rome and Constantinople" (CW 175).

It is noteworthy that Rudolf Steiner used varying terminology when speaking about the historical Manichaeism or the Manichaeism of the future. We find the following nomenclature:

Der Manichäismus—Manichaeism
Das Manichäertum
Das Manichäerprinzip—the Manichaean principle
   (CW 104, June 25, 1908)
Die Manichäerrichtung—the Manichaean orientation

Die Manichäische (Geistes)strömung—the
Manichaean (spiritual) stream (CW 93)
Der Manichäerorden—the Manichaean order (CW 96,
August 29, 1906)
Das Mani-Prinzip—the Mani principle (CW 104, June
25, 1908)
Mani / Manes

Manes is a Latinized version of *Mani.** It has not yet with
certainty been determined what the possible meanings are
of the name *Mani.* The full name is supposed to have been
Manichayya, a Syriac/Aramaic word. *Chayya* means "life, the
one who lives."

RUDOLF STEINER'S SOURCES

Concerning Rudolf Steiner's statements on Mani and
Manichaeism, there is only one source of which we can be certain that he had it at his disposal. It is mentioned in the endnotes
for the November 11, 1904, lecture in *The Temple Legend*
(CW 93): "Eugen Heinrich Scmitt (1851–1916), *Die Gnosis:
Grundlagen der Weltanschauung einer edleren Kultur*; vol. 1
[Gnosis: Fundamentals of the World View of a Noble Culture
and Gnosis in Antiquity]; *Die Gnosis des Altertums,* and vol.
2, *Die Gnosis des Mittelalters und der Neuzeit* [Gnosis in the
Middle Ages and in Modern Time], Scientia Verlag, Aalen,
reprinted 1968." Schmitt was born in Austria-Hungary and
became known as a pacifist, anarchist, and anti-clerical.

His book is in the Rudolf Steiner Archive in Dornach. In
the chapter on Manichaeism, Steiner had marked a few passages, including an extensive passage on the Manichaean creation myth that he called "a great cosmic legend" and of which
he gave a free rendition in his own words in the lecture of
November 11, 1904. He also marked a passage on the dispute

---

*   In this edition we have consistently used the name *Mani,* even when *Manes*
was used in texts quoted.

between the Manichaean bishop Faustus and St. Augustine. The references to these marked passages can be found in the endnotes to the lecture mentioned.

The notes begin with some general remarks about the text of the lecture. It may be important to look at these, especially since this is the sole lecture that Rudolf Steiner devoted entirely to Manichaeism. The text as we have it is based on shorthand notes by Franz Seiler and notes by Mathilde Scholl and Marie Steiner-von Sivers. The final version, however, appears to be a summary:

> All sources concur that we are here dealing with a short-ened version of this lecture. The conclusion especially is preserved in only a very fragmentary fashion. In a hand-written copy of the notes of Mathilde Scholl there is a marginal reference to the fact that the contents of this lec-ture were later included in the third degree of the section dealing with cult and symbolism of the Esoteric School. The main value that these notes have for us today is that they form the only full account of Manichaeism in the whole of Rudolf Steiner's work.[26]

Rudolf Steiner's library also contains the work of Joseph Schauberg, *Vergleichendes Handbuch der Symbolik der Freimaurerei mit besonderer Rücksicht auf die Mythologien und Mysterien des Altertums* (Comparative Compendium of the Symbolism of Freemasonry with Special Consideration of the Mythologies and Mysteries of Antiquity). The fact that those who have the degree of Master in Freemasonry call them-selves "Sons of the Widow" seems to connect Freemasonry with the legend of Mani as the son of a widow.

The endnotes to the lecture of November 11, 1904, also refer to two well-known publications of Steiner's time. These are the works of Franz Cument who wrote about the doctrine and cult of Mithras and who viewed Manichaeism as a continua-tion of the Mithras mysteries, and of Hans Heinrich Schaeder,

Origin and Development of the Manichaean System, lectures of 1924 to 1925 of the Warburg Library, Leipzig-Berlin 1927. Schaeder wrote: "We do not know what 'Son of the Widow' means." Rudolf Steiner spoke about this expression in more depth in lectures of February 1913.[27] Neither Cument's nor Schaeder's book is in Rudolf Steiner's library; however, in view of their influence in the academic world at the time it is quite possible that he was familiar with them.

St. Augustine and Other Church Fathers

Several Church Fathers have written treatises on Manichaeism: St Augustine (incl. *Contra Faustum, De natura boni, De moribus Manichaeorum*); Epiphanius of Salamis (*Panarion*); Hegemonius (*Acta Archelai*, [ed. C. H. Beeson, Leipzig, 1906]); Alexander of Lycopolis and Theodor bar Konai (*Liber Scholiorum*, book xi).

The Greek anti-Manichaean literature includes a document from the hand of Alexander of Lycopolis, probably written around the year 300.[28] According to Andrea Piras, Lycopolis' intention was not in the first place to refute Manichaean dogma, but to reject its doctrine on the basis of its mythical and suggestive character: "a myth applied by Manichaeans in a psych-agogical sense" (meaning to educate and uplift the soul).[29] Alexander of Lycopolis wrote that Mani taught two principles: God and matter, good and evil. The good is superior to evil (*Contra Manichaeos*).

Between 326 and 330 the *Acta Archelai* were written; these are attributed to Hegemonius and give a fictitious report of a discussion between a bishop named Archelaus and Mani. Here also we find the Manichaean doctrine of two gods, Light and Darkness, with darkness and matter being one and the same. Only the soul participates in the light because it is a fragment of the light.

At the end of the same century the *Panarion* was published, the "medicine cabinet" of Epiphanius of Salamis who wrote an extensive report on the Manichaeans. He also suggests that Manichaean dualism essentially boils down to a doctrine of two gods of which one is called God and the other the devil.

Among the Syrian writings the *Liber Scholiorum* by the Nestorian bishop from Kaskar, Theodor bar Konai (late eighth century), stands out because it offers a rather complete and detailed review of Mani's cosmogony.[30] In chapter 11, Bar Konai gives an elaborate account of the drama of primal man who is seized by the darkness, and of the resulting creation. The story begins with the Manichaean teaching of the two principles—Bar Konai called them "natures"—that existed even before the creation took place. The fact that this book was written in Syriac, a language closely related to Aramaic, opens the possibility that Bar Konai used expressions that literally go back to Mani's terminology.[31]

A late document from Zoroastrian circles, the *Skand-gumanik wizar*, the purpose of which was to refute the other religions as heresies, also contains a chapter with references to the Manichaean myth and creation story.

From the tenth and eleventh centuries we have the writings of Ibn al-Nadim, al-Biruni and Shahrestani. Among these the *Fihrist* by al-Nadim, a literary catalog drawn up in Baghdad in 988, has been without any doubt the most influential. In a commentary on the dualistic doctrine of Mani, al Nadim deviated from the usual terminology that speaks of principles or natures. He used the term *kawnan*, plural of *il-kawn*, which means "beings or things that are."

Shahrestani did not speak in his own name but referred to a Manichaean, Abu Isa al-Warraq, a former Zoroastrian who had converted to Manichaeism and knew it well. He described Mani's dualism as the teaching of the two principles that have existed from all eternity and will never cease to exist. They are each other's opposite as regards their essence, their form, their actions, and their effects. Remarkably, he interprets both natures as potencies equipped with the capacities of sense observation.

Standard Works in German

Here we will mention some standard works that, during the nineteenth and early twentieth centuries, laid the foundation for the scientific study of Manichaeism in the German-speaking world, and that as such became widely known. A list of these works can be found in the bibliography at the end of this book.

Although he wrote in French, we begin with the Huguenot Isaac de Beausobre (1659–1738), who is viewed as the founder of the modern, scientific study of Manichaeism. "We may rightfully consider the *Histoire* as the beginning of the modern science of Manichaeism."[32] This *Histoire critique de Manichée et du Manichéisme*, the two volumes of which appeared in Amsterdam in 1734 and 1739 respectively, demonstrates a critical attitude regarding the sources, which were in this work presented in an organized fashion for the first time. "...We may consider this work as a remarkable accomplishment of a unique quality, especially in comparison with what his contemporaries have written..." (ibid.). De Beausobre raised the question of the authenticity of the *Acta Archelai* as an important source of information on Manichaeism, and he showed that it is, in his opinion, a falsification.

It would take almost another hundred years (1831) before another study would see the light of day: *Das Manichaeische Religionssystem nach den Quellen neu untersucht und entwickelt* (The Manichaean Religious System Newly Researched and Developed from the Sources). The author was the theologian Ferdinand Christian Baur who focused on the dualistic doctrine in Mani's cosmogony and on his Christology. In his opinion, Manichaeism is not a heresy, but deserves a place in the history of religions. Baur also discussed the influences of Indian and Buddhist doctrines on Manichaeism.[33]

Gustav Flügel[34] (1862, 1871) and Konrad Kessler[35] (1889) made new material available with their publications and translations of Arabic historians and encyclopedists. Flügel is credited with the publication of the first Arabic edition of al-Nadim's *Fihrist*, in which he added notes and comments to the part about Mani's teaching. Shahrestani's *Encyclopedia* had already appeared in German in 1850, including a chapter on Mani, his family, his teaching, and his position relative to other prophets.[36] Flügel also discussed the concordance between these two authors who, together with al-Biruni, may be considered as the most important Arabic sources. The availability of the *Fihrist* also highlighted the problem of the differences between, on the one hand, the views of the Arabic historians of the origins of Mani and his doctrine, and those of the Church Fathers on the other.

Konrad Kessler no longer considered Manichaeism as a false doctrine but as an autonomous religion, and gave it a place in the complex Babylonian-Persian context of his time. In this regard, Kessler referred to Mani as a genius in the way he incorporated his teaching into the then existing moral and religious codes and their use of language and terminology. This also introduced the theme of Manichaeism as syncretism, a mixture of streams and insights. Finally, we mention Adolf von Harnack who called attention to the origin and development of Mani's dualism in an Assyrian-Babylonian context.[37]

RUDOLF STEINER AND MANICHAEAN TEACHING

The Question of Dualism

If we want to go further than just providing a summary of historical facts and data, the question of the nature of Mani's dualism is of essential importance. A better understanding of this dualism makes it possible to accord to the message of Mani the place it deserves among the multiple Gnostic-dualistic streams that were still current in his time.

Characteristics of Mani's Dualism

- First of all, Mani's dualism is radical. Both principles stand opposite to each other so that their difference can never be diminished, let alone be resolved.
- Mani's dualism is extreme. Both principles are in every respect of their essence opposed to each other in equal manner and in equal measure.
- Consequently, Mani's dualism is essential. In other words, this is an opposition between two creative principles, radical and extreme; their opposition lies in the very essence of the two principles.
- Mani's dualism is "horizontal." It is not an opposition between two principles that would each have a different rank (higher or lower), but two principles that belong to one and the same rank, albeit that they are each other's counter pole.
- Mani's dualism is dynamic. Both principles go through a process of change in the course of which the interaction between them changes, but not in the extent and the manner of their opposition.

It is evident that Mani's dualism demonstrates a clear nature of its own in many respects. What can we conclude from this?

- Mani's dualism distinguishes itself from many forms of Gnostic dualism because it accords equivalent positions to light and dark. Its dualism is horizontal, not vertical.[38] The light is not a higher principle but stands on equal footing with the darkness.

- But what distinguishes Mani's creation story most clearly from other forms of dualism is its dynamic aspect. Both principles do not rest in their opposition. This state of rest-in-themselves was the case only in the first era of non-interference. From the second era on, both principles enter into ever-stronger interaction with each other. In the *Shabuhragan* this is called the era of *gumezishn*, mingling. This mingling of both substances is a special characteristic of Mani's dualism.

- The immediate consequence of this is that, from this mingling, a substance is created that ultimately becomes matter. The *Shabuhragan* clearly describes how the beings of light and darkness are to the very last moment engaged in intense interaction with each other, of which matter is the result. This interaction is described in most realistic terms—essentially, that the beings of darkness devour the light beings. In other words, the mingling of light and darkness is a gigantic metabolic process in which one substance takes and integrates the other into itself.

The cosmological fragments of the *Shabuhragan* further describe how the beings of darkness that have already absorbed light elements, constantly copulating, mingle together more and more under the leadership of Az (which literally means "uncontrolled desire"). Obviously, this should not be taken literally; it should be understood as a metaphor for the ever-increasing proliferation of the mingled substance. In this process, Az herself will intervene a number of times and mix herself—i.e., her being, indicated in the text as *gryw* meaning soul, with plants and herbs that continue to carry a certain amount of light substance in them. Occasionally she hurtles down with the intention of potentizing the mingling process.

Mani's View of Matter

If matter is the end product, originating from the constant entanglement of light and darkness, this will lead us to the conclusion that in this conception matter cannot simply be equated with the powers of darkness. The question this necessarily raises is the question of the status of the two primal principles: light and darkness. In Manichaean horizontal dualism these principles occupy equal ranks in their essential being, but are opposed to each other in their nature. Occupying equal ranks means that they equally participate in the creation process. Without the interaction and interplay between light and darkness, no creation would have been able to take place. Darkness, with all the beings that inhabit it, would not by itself have been capable of creating the world and the human being. The collaboration of the light beings was necessary for this, under the leadership of Ormuzd, the Light Soul, who in the beginning entered into the darkness.

This leads us to the following:

- Light and Darkness are both necessary to the creation process.
- Creation, therefore, is not the work of dark forces, neither that of an evil Demiurge as in certain Gnostic creation myths.
- By contrast, in the Manichaean creation myth the Demiurge is a light being; in other words, the creation is a positive event.
- Matter appears at the end of creation as the product of the collaboration between light and darkness. They both take part in it, albeit each in accordance with its own nature.
- By definition therefore, matter is not in itself evil.
- Light and Darkness are both creative beings.

Rudolf Steiner on the
"Spirit–Matter Principle" in Manichaeism

From the quotations that follow, it is evident that Rudolf Steiner considered the split of spirit and matter, with which we are familiar in our time, as an achievement of the modern scientific thinking that developed in the West since the sixteenth and seventeenth centuries and reached a sort of culmination in the nineteenth century. This modern interpretation of the dichotomy of spirit and matter cannot, according to Steiner, be extrapolated back to the Manichaeans. Here follow statements by Steiner that point in the same direction:

> What is called at present the teaching of Mani is only the degenerate outcome of an ancient teaching that conceived the spirit only as creative and knew no difference between matter and spirit. No spirit was existent that did not create, and what it created was seen by the human being as matter. Just as little conception did these ancient times have of mere matter; on the contrary, spirit existed in everything.[39]

> We have to recognize that in Manichaeism people still strived to experience the lively mutual interpenetration of the spiritual world and the sense world. Those who adhered to the teaching of Mani absolutely wanted to view the sense world in such a way that, in every physical fact, in every physical thing, the spiritual can also be perceived; in other words, in the light, they also wanted to find wisdom and goodness, because they did not want to separate nature from pure spirituality. Spirit and nature were to be viewed as one. That was later called dualism—dualism because one could no longer bring together the two—spirit and nature—which one had once separated, whereas these were earlier viewed as a living unity.[40]

The first and most remarkable thing about it is that the division of human experience into a spiritual and a material side had no meaning for it. The words or ideas "spirit" and "matter" convey no distinction to it. It sees the spiritual in what appears to the senses as material, and when it speaks of the spiritual it does not rise above what manifests itself to the senses. (CW 74)

Rudolf Steiner on the Manichaean Cosmogony

In his lecture of November 11, 1904 (in *The Temple Legend*, CW 93), Rudolf Steiner sketched Mani's cosmogony. He introduced it as a legend, just like the Temple Legend, about which he had spoken in prior meetings, because spiritual streams that are connected with initiation express themselves exoterically by means of legends, he said. In the case of the Manichaean creation myth, we have a "great cosmic legend, a suprasensory legend."

[The legend] tells us that, at one time, the spirits of darkness wanted to take the kingdom of light by storm. They actually reached the borders of the kingdom of light and hoped to conquer it. But they failed to achieve anything. Now they were to be punished—and that is a very significant feature that I beg you to take account of—they were to be punished by the kingdom of light. But in this realm there was nothing that was in any way evil; there was only good. Thus the demons of darkness could have been punished only with something good. So what happened? The following: the spirits of light took a part of their own kingdom and mixed it with the materialized kingdom of darkness. Because there was now a part of the kingdom of light mingled with the kingdom of darkness, a leaven had been introduced into the kingdom of darkness—a ferment that produced a chaotic whirling dance, whereby it received a new element into itself: death. Therefore, it continually consumes itself and thus carries within itself the seed of its own destruction. It is further related that, just because of this, the human race was brought into existence. Primeval humankind represents just what was sent down from the kingdom of light to mix with the kingdom of darkness and to conquer, through death, what should not have been there; to conquer it with its own being.

Right after this description Steiner continued with an interpretation of the Manichaean creation myth:

The profound thought that lies in this is that the kingdom of darkness had to be overcome by the kingdom of light, not by means of punishment, but through mildness; not by resisting evil, but by uniting with it in order to redeem evil as such. Because a part of the light enters into evil, the evil itself is overcome.

In the same lecture Steiner compared "the interaction of good and evil" with what he called "the harmonization of life and form." Life can take on form only because form resists life and the other way around—form can bring itself to expression only by pushing back against life. In this interaction, through which living form, or formed life, can manifest, Steiner saw an analogy with the collaboration between light and darkness in the Manichaean creation myth as represented by him.

The Manichaean Creation Myth
and Its Rendering by Rudolf Steiner

Given the many, very different, sources on which a study of historical Manichaeism can be based in the early twenty-first century, it is possible to put together quite a complete picture of the Manichaean creation story. But one will also notice different nuances, depending on the context in which this part of the teaching is given. In addition, it is in this regard without a doubt important that only a few fragments of Mani's canonical works have been preserved. For instance, except for a few quotations and fragments, his *Living Gospel* and *Thesaurus* are virtually completely lost.

The only document from the hand of Mani himself in which he himself explained his system is the *Shabuhragan*, which he composed by order of King Shapur I. It is therefore possible that differing variations on the creation story have developed depending on the cultural-religious context of the time when they were written. This would explain why the Iranian-Chinese *Manichaica* shows differences with the Coptic *Manichaica*. The latter speaks of creation days and nights in which a shift takes place that gives the kingdom of light an advantage over the kingdom of darkness. We do not find such an "unevenness" in the Iranian Manichaean tradition.

Rudolf Steiner's rendering of Manichaean cosmogony, the only one in which he dealt with the subject at length, evokes a number of questions. First, there is the question of his possible external sources. As has been mentioned before, in the beginning of the twentieth century a number of basic works were already available of which the creation story formed part. Still, he can only have known (longer) quotations from the works of opponents of Manichaeism, or from the Persian and Arabic historians. It is not improbable that Steiner's rendition of the creation myth is based on the version of Ibn Nadim in the *Fihrist* or that of Theodor bar Khonai.

In addition, Steiner introduced elements into Manichaean cosmogony that have no precedent in the sources that were available in his time and that related different versions of the creation story. Whether Steiner had "other sources" at his disposal will remain an unanswered question. At this time we don't have any indications from his hand that would indicate other sources.

First and foremost, there is the element that the powers of the realm of darkness were unable to accomplish anything against the realm of light. "But they failed to achieve anything." Also the punishment of the realm of darkness by the realm of light turns out to be an addition by Steiner. The mingling of light and darkness can indeed be found in the sources, but Steiner places the initiative for this exclusively in the light realm. Finally, the statement that this mingling results in the introduction of a new element into the realm of darkness, namely death, is probably unique to Steiner. It is indeed correct that by the mingling a change occurs at the level of substance. The mingling *is* in fact this new substance. Steiner's interpretation agrees closely with the sources when he related that primal human was sent by the light realm into the realm of darkness. Which side took the initiative for the mingling remains open to differing interpretations. But the introduction of the new element of death is not explicitly mentioned in the sources.

Rudolf Steiner on Dualism and Manichaean Dualism

What meets us in the world outside presents itself to us in contrasts, antitheses; it is truly dualistic. In this respect Manichaeism, when correctly understood in its dualism, is fully justified. How this Manichaeism is fully justified also within a spiritual monism is something we will be able to discuss more than once in the future.[41]

The above quote not only gives us one of Steiner's interpretations of Mani's dualism, we also read about Steiner's most personal view of dualism versus monism. One could call it a dynamic view. What meets us from the world we observe presents itself to us as a contrast. Steiner dealt with this in his book *The Philosophy of Freedom* (or *Intuitive Thinking as a Spiritual Path*). A kind of dualism exists in which both poles can never meet. Each remains itself, and an unbridgeable chasm exists between them.

"Dualism... feels that there must be a bridge between the two worlds but is not in a position to find it."[42] However, there is also a dualism in which the tension between the two poles, caused by their absolute opposition, is transformed into a dynamic of interaction. The interaction expresses itself in a momentary neutralizing of the duality. In that moment we have monism, not the usual rigid monism, but a dynamic monism.

In thinking that becomes conscious of itself, the separation between "I" and the world, or between subject and object, is lifted for the duration of this thinking. "The activity exercised by man as a *thinking* being is thus not merely subjective. Rather it is something neither subjective nor objective that transcends both these concepts."[43] True, out of this monism a new duality will arise but, on condition that this duality remains dynamic, the possibility remains of a new moment of mutual interaction. In *The Philosophy of Freedom*, Steiner places the moment of dualism on the side of perceiving consciousness for it is in the process of perception that we place ourselves opposite the world and from which we form concepts. This dualism is only lifted when we bring the process of thinking itself to consciousness.

In the Manichaean creation story, the tension between light and darkness leads to darkness engaging the light realm in battle. In other words, a dynamic is born from this radical dualism that results in a mingling. This is not a tragic mingling in the sense of a fall into the abyss of matter. On the contrary, this mingling opens the possibility of transforming the creation into a new condition, in which all created things will appear as transfigured in all their glory of light. In this connection we can also understand Steiner's statement in which he, looking in the direction of the Mani intention, spoke of a "wonderful and lofty" principle. "Although at the present day this principle of Mani has had to step very much into the background because there is little understanding for spiritual work, this wonderful and lofty Manichaean principle will win more and more pupils the nearer we approach the understanding of spiritual life."[44]

Rudolf Steiner and the Individuality of Mani

Whenever we read statements by Rudolf Steiner about the individuality of Mani, we have to distinguish different aspects from each other. First and foremost, there is the historical information, which Steiner categorizes as "outer history." Thus, in the lecture of November 11, 1904, he sketched a biography of Mani in which he more or less related what is described about Mani's life in the *Acta Archelai*. In this connection he also used the expression "son of the widow." Moreover, Steiner also mentioned the fact that Mani considered himself to be the *Paraclete*. Finally, he called Mani a "high ambassador of Christ."

Rudolf Steiner and the Acta Archelai

The *Acta Archelai* is an anti-Manichaean document written around the middle of the fourth century by a certain Hegemonius. It was incorporated into the *Panarion* (literally: medicine cabinet; to cure diseases of heresy), a document written by Epiphanius of Salamis. In Latin translation, the *Panarion* spread over Western Europe. Until the discoveries in the early twentieth century, it was often, but not always, viewed as a reliable document, so that it was used as the basis of a study of Mani and Manichaeism. Rudolf Steiner evidently referred to such studies when he said in his lecture of November 11, 1904: "What outer history has to say about Mani is very simple."

When Steiner gave this lecture, the biographical sketch in the *Fihrist* by Ibn al Nadim was also known, but this limits itself much more strictly to the then-known historical information.

We first quote Rudolf Steiner's words and then give a summary of the texts of the *Acta Archelai* to the extent there are parallels with Steiner.

44

It is said that there once lived a merchant in the Near East who was very learned. He compiled four important works: first, *Mysteria*, secondly, *Capitola*, thirdly, *Evangelium*, and lastly, *Thesaurus*. It is further related that at his death he left these works to his widow who was a Persian. This widow, on her part, left them to a slave whose freedom she had bought and whom she had liberated. That was the said Mani, who then drew his wisdom out of these writings, though he was also initiated into the Mithraic mysteries. Mani is called the "Son of the Widow" and his followers are called the "Sons of the Widow." (CW 93)

From the *Acta Archelai* (summary):

A man called Skythianos, a Saracen, lived in the time of the apostles in Scythia [southern Russia] and traveled to Egypt, where he absorbed the wisdom of the Egyptians and wrote this down in scriptures, namely in the four books with the titles *Mysteria*, *Kephalaia*, *Evangelium*, and *Thesaurus*. Subsequently he went to Palestine, and when he died these documents came into the hands of a certain Terebinthus, who went to Babylon where he had a widow as his pupil. Later he would call himself Buddha. When he, too, died, because he fell from the roof to the ground, the wisdom books became the possession of the widow. This woman had a young slave named Corbicius. When Corbicius was twelve years old and the widow sensed her approaching death, she granted him freedom and gave him the four wisdom books. He changed his name to Mani, studied the wisdom in the books, and began to preach his teaching from these books.

Generally speaking, Steiner appears to have based himself on the well-known story from the *Acta Archelai*—namely the existence of four wisdom books and the fact that these were at a certain moment given by a widow to her young slave. The expression "Son of the Widow," to which we will return later, is not mentioned in the *Acta*, nor is the fact that the young slave was said to have been initiated in the Mithras mysteries. Nor does Steiner mention the names Skythianus, Terebinthus, and Corbicius.

It is clear that the *Acta Archelai*, like so many apologetic writings, shows a mixture of truth and falsification. However, if we were to reject it as entirely false, we would ignore a number of interesting elements. The most striking of these is that the titles of the four wisdom books are the same as those of the four canonical scriptures of Mani himself. In a passage we have not quoted, the *Acta* mentions later pupils of Mani, including Thomas and Adda, in complete agreement with the tradition. Finally, the fact that we are told Corbicius receives these scriptures when he is twelve years old is a clear reference to an initiation event.

In the opinion of some researchers, an existing Mani legend could have formed the basis for what was to live on in the writings of his opponents as falsification and ridicule of Mani's life.[45] In the original Mani legend, mention of Egypt and later Palestine (especially Jerusalem) could have indicated that Mani wished to place himself in a certain tradition.

A Second Version

Rudolf Steiner's lecture of November 11, 1904 (as reported in *The Temple Legend*), is based on shorthand and longhand notes made by three persons who were present at the lecture. The endnote says: "All sources concur that we are here dealing with a shortened version of this lecture." Rudolf Steiner is said to have related the same legend in a lecture to a group of members (no date and place indicated). It is interesting to include the literal transcript of this second version here:

> Mani, or Manes, the founder of Manichaeism, appeared in the third century CE in Babylon. An unusual legend

has the following to say about him: Skythianus and Terebinthus or Buddha, were his predecessors. The latter was the pupil of the former. After the violent death of Skythianus, Terebinthus fled with the books to Babylon. He also suffered misfortune; the only one to accept his teaching was an elderly widow. She inherited his books and left them, at her death, to her foster child, a twelve-year-old boy whom she had adopted out of slavery when he was seven years old. The latter, who might also be called a "Son of a Widow," came to public notice at the age of twenty-four as Mani, the founder of Manichaeism. (CW 93, endnote 8, Nov. 11, 1904)

The same endnote refers to D. Schwolsohn, *Die Sabier und der Sabismus*, 1856, and quotes at length the legend as described and commented on in that book.

The Son of a Widow

While in the *Acta Archelai* Corbicius, who would later call himself Mani, is called the slave, and not the son, of the widow, Rudolf Steiner interpreted this in an esoteric sense. Nevertheless, one can also interpret this expression in a broader sense, namely that the term "the son of a widow" here means that the "father principle" is not present. In other words, there is no transmission (teaching and handing on) from teacher to pupil as regards the achievement of esoteric wisdom. A "son of a widow" is someone who begins to school himself in wisdom on his own, out of his own forces.

From sources that were discovered later, such as the Coptic *Homilies*, we know that Mani himself, when he justified himself in his last interview with King Vahram, claimed: "I have neither master nor teacher." In other texts, including the Turfan fragment M 5794, Mani distances himself from former prophets, teachers, and apostles by solemnly proclaiming with great emphasis: "My wisdom, my truth, my religion, my knowledge, my scriptures."

My chosen religion is in tenfold ways greater and better than the religions of former founders. To begin with, the religions of the predecessors were spread in only one land and in one language. My religion, however, is of such a nature that it will be known everywhere and in all languages and will be taught also in distant regions.... Because of its holy scriptures, its bishops and teachers, her *electi* and her *auditors*, and because of its wisdom and deeds, my religion will endure to the end of time. The revelation of the two principles (light and darkness), my living scriptures, my truth and my knowing are more encompassing than those of the earlier religions.[46]

In both chapter 76 and chapter 38 of the *Kephalaia*, Mani calls himself the one and only, solitary Mani. He even literally says, "Imagine that there had been two Manis! The world would not have been able to carry their weight!"

Mani and the Paraclete

Further to what "outer history" tells about Mani, Rudolf Steiner went on to speak about the extraordinary relationship that Mani claimed to have with the Paraclete. The fact that Mani saw himself as the Paraclete is also mentioned in the *Acta Archelai*. In Steiner's words:

Mani described himself as the "Paraclete," the Holy Spirit promised to humankind by Christ. We should understand by this that he saw himself as *one* incarnation of the Holy Spirit; he did not mean that he was the *only* one. He explained that the Holy Spirit reincarnated, and that he was one such reincarnation. (CW 93)

There are also other sources that mention similar statements. An important one in this regard is Mani's speech to his pupils in the *Kephalaia of the Teacher* (4–9). In this address to his pupils, Mani first mentions the Paraclete, referring to the words of the Gospel: "Him of whom the Savior has said:

I shall send you the Paraclete." Mani then unfolds, step by step, the connection between the Paraclete and his *syzygos* (his higher self) and finally, that between his *syzygos*-Paraclete and himself, Mani. "From that moment [namely the beginning of Mani's public appearance] the Paraclete, the Spirit of Truth, was sent to you." After this he goes a step further and says: "In the same year when Ardashir, the King, was about to be crowned, the living Paraclete came to me and spoke to me" (*Kephalaia of the Teacher*, 31–32).

The identification with the Paraclete is pursued even further when Mani in the same address declares how his *syzygos* and the Paraclete are one and the same. By this *syzygos*-Paraclete, says Mani, "I have known everything, and by him I have seen the All, and with him I became one, in body and in spirit" (ibid., 24).

Mani's Spiritual Stature and Rank

Rudolf Steiner spoke about the spiritual stature of Mani only with the greatest reluctance. In Mani he recognized a high spiritual individuality sent by Christ as a teacher of humanity, and whose task he formulated in the quotation below as "transforming the powers of evil." Mani saw himself as a prophet and an apostle. As prophet he had the task to promulgate to the world the content of the mysteries— i.e., what was revealed to him by his Twin Self. He was not just a prophet; Mani viewed himself as the last in the series of great prophets who preceded him. That is why the title was given him that was later also given to the prophet Mohammed: "The Seal of the Prophets."

> Mani is that exalted individuality who is repeatedly incarnated on the Earth, who is the guiding spirit of those whose task it is to transform evil. When we speak of the great leaders of humankind, we must also think of this individuality who has set himself this task.

Although at the present day this principle of Mani has had to step very much into the background because there is little understanding of spiritual work, the wonderful and lofty Manichaean principle will win more and more pupils the nearer we approach the understanding of spiritual life. (CW 104)

On the theme "son of the widow" and on Mani's prior incarnations we have notes made by Elisabeth Vreede without indication of place and date. She reported that the youth of Nain, a son of a widow, whose raising from death by Christ is related in the Gospel of St. Luke (7:11–17), was a prior incarnation of Mani.

> ... a boy of twelve years whom she adopted when he was seven years old (as a slave) in place of her own son. Her adopted son, who can also be called the "Son of a Widow," appeared at the age of twenty-four as Mani, the founder of Manichaeism....
>
> This soul that formerly lived in the Young Man of Nain was engaged in preparation; he was initiated in this way by Christ for a future when the contents of Manichaeism, which have not yet fully developed, will arise for the salvation of the people of the ancient East. During his life as Mani this soul worked to prepare for his real future mission: to bring about the true reconciliation of all religions.
>
> To achieve this he had to be born again as a soul with a very special relationship to the Christ.... He was born again as Parsifal, the son of Herzeleide...[47]

In his lecture cycle on the Gospel of St. Luke, Steiner did not refer to Mani, but he did speak about different forms of initiation and said:

> In another kind of initiation it is only a seed that is implanted into the soul, and the individual has to wait until the next incarnation for the seed to bear fruit; only

then does he become an initiate in the true sense. The initiation of the Young Man of Nain was of this kind.[48]

Albert Steffen, in his drama *The Death Experience of Manes*, let Mani look back to a former earthly life as the Youth of Nain. In response to a question to Rudolf Steiner by Walter Johannes Stein as to the individuality of Parsifal, Mani is mentioned as one who stands even higher than Zarathustra and Skythianos (W. J. Stein, *The Ninth Century*).

Ehrenfried Pfeiffer referred in a lecture of December 22, 1946, to social threefolding as "a preparatory work for a future incarnation of Mani." He further quoted Rudolf Steiner's words in this connection, that both Waldorf pedagogy and the threefold social order are prerequisites for this incarnation to take place, so that a "fitting body" can be prepared for it.

> Mani will not incarnate during this [twentieth] century, but intends to do so in the next century, if he can find a suitable body. The ordinary kind of education does not provide any possibility for Mani to develop; only Waldorf education would do so. If the right conditions are provided he will appear as a teacher of humankind and take up leadership in matters of art and religion. He will act from the power of the Grail Mysteries, and he will instruct humankind so that they may decide even about good and evil.[49]

Finally, in the final lecture of the cycle *The East in the Light of the West*, Rudolf Steiner spoke of a meeting of three great initiates, namely Skythianos, Zarathustra, and Buddha, who were called together by Mani. Rudolf Steiner called this a council in the spiritual world. About Mani he said the following:

> There is a fourth individuality named in history, behind whom, for those who have the proper comprehension, much lies hidden—an individuality still higher and more

powerful than Skythianos, the Buddha, or Zarathustra. This individuality is Mani, and those who see more in Manichaeism than is usually the case know him to be a very high messenger of Christ.... Mani called these persons together to consult with them as to the means of reintroducing the wisdom that had lived through the changing times of the post-Atlantean age and of causing it to unfold more and more gloriously in the future.[50]

In this connection, Skythianos, Buddha, and Zarathustra can also be understood as representatives of what is in human nature the physical body, the life body, and the consciousness organization. Mani, the fourth and highest among these initiates and teachers of humanity, represents the human "I." As will be discussed later, it is the human "I" that can have part in both good and evil. In other words, the transformation of the powers of evil in the future can only be brought about in and by the "I." This is also an important aspect of the Mani intention.

3

THE MISSION OF EVIL: RUDOLF STEINER AND THE MANI INTENTION

"The members of the Manichaean Order are already learning how to transform quite radically those who by nature are wholly evil. Then the transformed evil will become a quite special good." (CW 95)

For Rudolf Steiner the future task of Manichaeism—what is here called the Mani intention—is a natural consequence of the way in which in Manichaeism the question of good and evil has its place in the whole cosmogony and anthropology of Mani. It is therefore necessary, according to Steiner, to develop a correct comprehension of this Manichaean view if one also wishes to understand the Mani intention. It should be noted that in the Manichaean creation myth the moral dimension acquires significance only in the moment when human beings become aware that they, too, were created from light and darkness. This insight, to which the customary term of "Gnosis" is applicable, concurrently creates the responsibility to act. Acquiring insight while not acting in accordance with it can only mean that either one lives in the illusion of having acquired insight, or that one refuses to act in agreement with the insight that, in itself, is already an expression of a moral intention.

Evil has a role to play in creation, said Steiner, who in this regard agrees with Manichaeism. It is not a phenomenon that came into being outside of the creation, or outside of the divine will, and that really should not have been there.

> The essence of Manichaean teaching relates to the doctrine of good and evil. In ordinary thought, good and evil are two irreducible qualities, one of which, goodness, must destroy the other, evil. To Manichaeans, however, evil is integral to the cosmos and collaborates in its evolution, and it will eventually be absorbed and transfigured by goodness. The great feature of Manichaeism is that it investigates the function of evil and suffering in the world. (CW 94)

This does not need to be grounds for pessimism. "These observations are not a reason for pessimism, but rather should serve to arouse us and stimulate us to action."[51]

Another point on which Rudolf Steiner was of like mind with the Manichaean view is that, as he clearly indicated in a number of lectures, the powers of evil are represented by spiritual beings.[52] In Manichaeism also, the *archontes* of the darkness are identified as spiritual beings who prove to possess creative capacities. In both cases, the point is that evil must not be equated with created matter.

Evil as Ill-Timed Good

Rudolf Steiner's lecture of November 11, 1904 (CW 93), takes us immediately into the core of the problem. It is the earliest known lecture on this subject and he spoke with emphasis of the Mani intention: "Manichaeism teaches that evil is just as eternal as good; that there is no resurrection of the body, and that evil, as such, will continue forever." Steiner referred here to the points of doctrine of good and evil on which Manichaeism differs from Catholic Christianity. He went on to speak about Manichaean cosmogony (see the quotation on page 39) and to conclude as follows:

> The profound thought that lies in this is that the kingdom of darkness has to be overcome by the kingdom of light, not by means of punishment, but through mildness; not by resisting evil, but by uniting with it in order to redeem evil as such.... What is evil? Nothing but an ill-timed good.... So we see that evil is nothing else than a misplaced good.[53]

Evil, therefore, was originally good but at a certain moment turned into its opposite. In this way even the divine, if it remains behind in its development, can "at the wrong moment" turn into evil.

Later in the same lecture, Steiner developed a parallel in this regard with the principles of form and life. He justified the parallel by showing that, if we wish to understand how good and evil can come to a collaboration, we must first develop an understanding of the way in which the collaboration between form and life comes about. A living being that develops over time, said Steiner, owes this development to the collaboration between the principles of form and life. We should understand the collaboration of the principles of light and darkness, of good and evil, in the same way. For instance, if the principle of life continues to operate where it is no longer appropriate, it will go haywire and create chaos. Form and life, as forming principles, can do no other than work together in the way good and evil also need to work together: "How do we imagine the interworking of good and evil? We have to explain it as the harmonization of life with form" (CW 93).

In the same lecture Rudolf Steiner brought the phrase "son of the widow" to the attention of his audience. The widow is the soul that has lost her spouse, as Isis lost Osiris. The child that is born from them is the *son of a widow* and, as Steiner said, must "find the light of the spirit in his own soul." And a little later: "Everything that comes from Mani is an appeal to man's own spirit light of soul, out of man's own observation of his soul" (CW 93).

In the so-called testament of Bernard Lievegoed, *The Battle for the Soul*, the task of the Manichaean stream is described as the development of mildness and love: "Developing gentleness towards evil, that is the great task on the path of Manichaeism. Gentleness and love are the forces that save the human soul."[54]

Manichaeism and the Future of Christianity: Form and Life

"What are Mani's intentions? What is the meaning of his statement that he is the Paraclete, the Spirit, the Son of the Widow?" (CW 93).

In these questions of Rudolf Steiner it looks as if the various aspects of the figure of Mani—Paraclete, Spirit, Son of the Widow—are pulled together into one single individuality. The answer Steiner formulated should be understood in the perspective of the Mani intention:

> It means no less than that he intends to prepare for the time when the people of the sixth [cultural epoch] will be guided from their own being, their own soul's light, to overcome outer forms and convert them into spirit. (CW 93)

The outer form that Steiner mentions here is the form that Christianity adopted in the fourth and fifth centuries, partially under the influence of St. Augustine. This form was needed so that the life of Christianity would not perish owing to a lack of form. However, these were outer forms—forms that had arisen in a life that flourished before Christianity, the time of the Roman culture. But the form that was derived from Roman culture is not the right one for the life of Christianity. It is a provisional form. Therefore, the future task of Manichaeism is to create a form in which Christianity can really come to life.

What is still waiting to be made is the form for the life of the sixth [cultural epoch]. That must be created beforehand; it has to be there so that Christian life can be poured into it.... And this external form of society must derive from the intention that Mani has fostered, from the small group that Mani has prepared. That must be the outer form of organization, the congregation in which the spark of Christianity will first be truly kindled. (CW 93)

The "I" as Double-Edged Sword

Rudolf Steiner began the eighth lecture of his cycle on the Apocalypse of St. John (Nuremberg, June 25, 1908, in CW 104) by reminding the audience that our seven cultural ages will end with the War of All against All and then explaining what the real cause of this war will be. What he then said is indeed shockingly evident: the origin of the increase in the working of evil in the world lies in the human "I," the human self. It is because the "I," to satisfy its own interest, denies a space to another "I." It is because the "I" appropriates the riches of the earth for its own gratification at the expense of the life circumstances of another "I." In brief, it is because the "I" is still to a large extent driven by egoism and self-interest. "Those who do not fully realize that this 'I' is a two-edged sword will scarcely be able to grasp the entire meaning of the evolution of humankind and the world."

In the human "I," which Steiner compared in this regard to the double-edged sword in the Book of Revelation, lives a twofold orientation: a gesture of integration and one of exclusion; a yes and a no. "To drive away all the other egos from its realm is one side of the 'I.' On the other hand, we must not forget that it is the 'I' that at the same time gives human beings independence and inner freedom, which in the truest sense of the word exalts humanity. Our dignity is founded in this 'I'; it is the basis of the divine in the human being."

What would be the meaning of a yes if it could not just as well have been a no? What is the meaning of love if it does not originate from the potential of freedom of the "I"? "No love is perfect if it proceeds from coercion, from people being chained together. Only when each ego is so free and independent that it need not love, is its love an entirely free gift."

This twofold potential, anchored in the "I," the spiritual core of human nature, is also our guarantee for the development of freedom. Without this potential we would turn into automatons and addicts of the good. The good would exist without the human being participating in it, and would therefore not be a true good. "It would amount to human beings being led by strings of dependence if they could in any way be forced to love, even if only to the slightest degree."

Only in the tension of the "I" standing between the possibilities of good and evil do we bring our humanity to its full realization, and this means nothing less than that we succeed in practicing an appropriate interplay between freedom and love. "Thus the 'I' will be the pledge for the highest goal of humankind. But, at the same time, if it does not discover love, if it hardens within itself, it is the tempter that plunges human beings into the abyss.... Consequently, it is a sharp, two-edged sword."

If we want to study evil, said Steiner, who here also referred to the task he described as the Mani intention, namely to study evil in its essence and in the way it works—if we want to study evil, the field of exploration is always right there for us. It suffices to take note of what is playing out in our own "I." In addition, still in the same lecture, Steiner placed the "I," with its potential toward good as well as evil, in the perspective of the further development of humanity. It is in this perspective that he placed the task of Manichaeism, when things will come to a climax in the sixth and seventh cultural epochs, to the War of All against All, and to a separation between the good and the bad.

Steiner mentioned it as a world-historical necessity that the powers of evil will be driven to the extreme. Only then do the powers of good receive the opportunity to develop further. "It is necessary in the great plan that evil, too, should come to a peak.... The good would not be so great a good if it were not to grow through the conquest of evil."

Steiner called the preparation for this situation the "great task of education" of the Manichaeans. He characterized Mani as the individuality who incarnates again and again on Earth, and who has shouldered the task of leading those who have undertaken to convert evil. Finally, Steiner concluded that this "Mani principle" in our time has been pushed into the background, because there is little understanding of spirituality. If, however, the understanding of spiritual life would grow, this principle of the Manichaeans would be able to gain more and more followers: "This wonderful and lofty Manichaean principle will win more and more pupils the nearer we approach the understanding of spiritual life."

Earlier in the lecture, Steiner had already stated that the final goal of Anthroposophy was to create the possibilities for a community in which every "I" can in freedom meet the other "I." It is one and the same possibility of the human "I" that is capable out of love "to overcome the wickedness in the countenances of evil human beings"—in other words, to fulfill the "Mani principle" in freedom and love through the "I."

Although Rudolf Steiner did not say it in so many words, Anthroposophy and Manichaeism come together on this point. The right understanding of the reality of the spiritual and the transformation of this understanding into a concrete approach to life clearly belong together.

Initiation into the Mystery of Evil

In October 1918, concurrently with the difficult ending of World War I, Rudolf Steiner gave a cycle of lectures in which he showed a relationship between the characteristics of a specific period of development and initiation principles that are operating in that period.[55] For our current epoch, which he characterized as the era of the consciousness soul, he mentions the principle of initiation into the mystery of evil. Although this initiation will not be completed until the following, the sixth, cultural epoch, it still means that as we assimilate the characteristics of the consciousness soul, we at the same time also develop "tendencies" toward every form of evil.

> Since the beginning of the fifth post-Atlantean epoch, evil tendencies are subconsciously present in all people.... There is not a crime in the calendar to which all human beings, insofar as they belong to the fifth post-Atlantean epoch, are not subconsciously prone.

The consequences of this assimilation of tendencies toward evil do not only exist where these tendencies are indeed converted into deeds. "Whether in a particular case this tendency leads to an evil action depends upon wholly different circumstances and not upon the tendency itself." We need to look elsewhere for the reason why the forces of evil have to be assimilated into the human being.

> Humankind beings must assimilate these forces of evil, which are operative in the universe. By doing so, we implant in our being the seed to experience consciously the life of the spirit.... These forces of evil do not exist in the universe for the sole purpose of inducing human beings to commit criminal acts [but] to enable us to break through to the life of the spirit at the level of the consciousness soul.

Although Steiner did not mention Manichaeism per se in these lectures, we hear an unmistakable "Manichaean undertone," as well as the clear presence of connections with Manichaean anthropology and the Mani intention.

The consciousness soul is characterized by the capacity to close itself off from its surroundings, which makes possible a personal path of liberation from social, cultural, and religious connections. The "I" becomes conscious of its potential, for instance, to exercise power over another "I" out of self-interest. But closing oneself off may also result in isolation, which in turn may cause feelings of anxiety and loneliness. The coin has two sides: emancipation and being thrown back on one's own. Still, said Steiner, "human beings must first pass through the stage of the consciousness soul if they wish to receive after their own fashion the forces of the spirit self, life spirit, and spirit body." Mark the words "after their own fashion." It means that the "I," as double-edged sword, can participate in this future development so that, because of the "I," freedom can become an integral part of the further path of humanity.

In agreement with the Manichaean view, Steiner described how the forces of evil are becoming continually stronger in the inner life of human beings. This is "initiation." The spiritual forces that reign in the world-all are becoming an integral part of the human "I." This then also opens the possibility that these forces of evil can be transformed and redeemed. Redemption is an event that can only take place from one being to another. Human beings are not capable of redeeming the powers of evil in the world-all. Only the Savior, the Redeemer, has that ability. But human beings have been given the capacity to get to know the powers of evil in themselves in such a way that a beginning of redemption becomes possible. The era of the consciousness soul marks the stage when a first beginning can be made in this direction. What counts for this is not any spectacular deeds, but it happens in the little daily vicissitudes of life.

In the same lecture, Rudolf Steiner spoke of practicing unconditional interest in our fellow human beings as the process through which we can learn to see others as they really are. "People still ignore the most important element in others;

they have no understanding of their neighbor." Nevertheless, "an important impulse in the epoch of the consciousness soul is the development of an active concern on the part of all for their neighbor."

Concern is not the same as interest. In the latter, self-interest still plays a role. True concern—interest that poses no conditions and does not expect results in the sense of reciprocity, is none other than an expression of the good, in which the "I" participates. Cultivating such concern as an ongoing inner condition demands great self-knowledge—knowledge and awareness of all the tendencies toward evil that I carry *in myself*. These are not really overcome in the practice of concern for others, but they are redeemed.

4

MANI AS ARTIST AND
THE SIGNIFICANCE OF ART
IN MANICHAEISM

Mani, All-around Artist

As interest in Manichaeism has been increasing starting in the early twentieth century, because of the discovery of original documents, the principal focus has been on the content of Mani's teaching, the historical particulars of his biography, the organization of his church, and on further developments of Manichaeism in East and West. In a certain sense, this emphasis has been the cause of the fact that an integral part of Manichaeism has been overlooked, namely the artistic talents of Mani himself and the role that art, in the widest sense of the word, was given within a Manichaean community. Nevertheless, a number of interesting studies and surveys of Manichaean art have appeared relating to the discoveries of the very first expeditions to the Turfan Oasis.[56] What is so far mostly lacking, however, is an exploration of the specific individual character of the role that art played in Mani's preaching as prophet and apostle.

Mani was himself the first to emphasize the importance of the artistic dimension, for instance, when he wrote that he did not only put the wisdom of his revelations down in words and writing, but also in pictures.

For the Apostles all, my Brothers, who before me came, [did not write down] their wisdom as I wrote mine, [nor did] they paint their wisdom in pictures as I [did] paint mine.[57]

Picture Book is the customary title for Mani's book of images. It is the work in which Mani presented the content of the creation myth in pictures. It is interesting that a later commentary from Mani's hand has been preserved, the *Ardahang Wifras,* that gives explanations to the pictures. Fragments of this commentary have been found in the Parthian language. A question we immediately have in connection with this work is what was meant with the word "picture." Are these illustrations of his teaching? The existence of a commentary to the Picture Book seems to contradict this, for here it is the word that "illustrates" the pictures!

Before going into this further, it is interesting to trace the role of art in Manichaeism. For in this regard we also run the risk that certain elements escape our notice. First, there are Mani's own statements in which he places the spoken and written word as having equal value side by side with the painted picture. In addition, owing to the discoveries in and around the Turfan Oasis, items that go back to the period between the eighth and fourteenth centuries, and that include miniature fragments, silk paintings,[58] and frescoes,[59] one might have the impression that Manichaean art consists exclusively of painted works. A contributing factor to this is certainly the circumstance that in the Iranian tradition Mani is viewed preeminently as a painter. We can see pictures of Mani at work as a painter in countless Persian miniatures, for instance, from the prime of the Safavid Empire in the sixteenth to eighteenth centuries. According to the Persian historian Bayanu 'l Adyan, a reliable source, there was at the end of the eleventh century a version of the *Picture Book* in Ghazna (now in Afghanistan) that formed part of the treasury of the then reigning dynasty:

Mani was able, so it is said, to paint such a perfect line on a piece of white silk that, when the thread was pulled out, the line also disappeared. He was the creator of a book with a number of pictures, which is called *Ardahang* [Picture Book]. It can be found in the treasury of Ghaznin.

In addition to his talents as a painter, Mani was also a poet and composer of music. He is said to have been the inventor of a musical instrument, a sort of lute. In the *Fihrist* by Ibn al-Nadim the title of one of Mani's letters has been preserved as *On the Excellence of Sacred Music*. The *Book of Psalms* from Medinet Madi mentions hymns and psalms that were composed by Mani. Also as preacher and proclaimer of the word Mani possessed a power that we might well compare with the "gift of the word" of St. Paul. All this leads us to understanding Mani not only as a painter, but as an all-round artist. An important element in the artistic aspect of Manichaeism was the way a community was organized, as well as the cult and rituals that took place in the community.

Although this can only be advanced as a kind of working hypothesis, it seems that Manichaeism never expressed itself in a particular style of architecture. The Manichaeans rather tended to make use of existing sacred spaces, which can be demonstrated with certainty in the meditation caves found along the Silk Road. There one and the same space was often used by Buddhists, Nestorian Christians, and Manichaeans. A Manichaean monastery, however, always consisted of five spaces or halls, but this was not an architectural characteristic; rather it was an expression of the organizational form of their community, which consisted of two principal sections, the *electi* and the *auditores*. The *electi* were those who had made the threefold vow of purity of word, deed, and inner disposition, and who distinguished themselves by their white dress from the laity that lived with their families in the surroundings. The group of *electi* were subdivided into 360 elders, seventy-two bishops, and twelve teachers with the thirteenth in their midst, the successor of Mani, who formed the center of the community. Both men and women could be *electi*, as is shown by the frescoes and miniature fragments from Turfan.

Five is not an arbitrary number for the Manichaeans, but an image of the sacrifice made by Primal Man, the "Living Light Soul" who, when he is devoured by the powers of darkness, had girded himself with five light elements. In the course of the process of creation, these five light elements are changed into five "instruments" for the inner transformation of the human being. Each of these elements can be transfigured into soul and spiritual instruments on the path to the eventual transformation of the Earth and humanity at the end of time.

The five halls of a Manichaean monastery not only form a picture of this, they bring it to life by continually bringing it to the consciousness of those who use the building.

The Ritual Meal as Prototype of Manichaean Art

The religious life of a Manichaean community centered on the daily ritual meal that was celebrated by the *electi* in the presence of the laity. It was celebrated as a cultic event. It was the task of the laity to grow and harvest the fruits and vegetables for this meal so that they could be prepared every day. But they were not permitted to participate in the meal, a fact that was more than once the subject of sharp criticism of Manichaeism by its apologists and opponents including, of course, St. Augustine who, according to his own words, was not allowed to attend the meal, which he called "Eucharist" (St. Augustine, *Contra Fortunatum*, 3).

The significance of this ritual can only be fully understood if it is viewed in relation to Mani's message as a whole. Food as substance is preeminently a very real picture of the mingling of light and darkness, the condition of humanity after the creation. The key idea was that taking in food as a mixed substance offered the possibility of separating light and darkness from each other again. A prerequisite for this was that the ones who took the meal would perfect themselves in a process of inner catharsis, in which they would be able to discern and identify the elements of light and darkness in themselves to such an extent, that each of them was restored to its own nature. The process of metabolism is also clearly a process of discernment and identification in which substances that are mixed together, in other words, in a condition of uncleanness, are each given back to themselves. The light, which in this way had regained its own nature, could then be taken up in the "Column of Glory," the place in the cosmos where the future light is collected in expectation of the complete illumination and transfiguration of the Earth.

It is important to understand that the point of this ritual is the transformation of the food as mixed earthly substance, not the transformation of the ones who consume the food. The *electi*, who took the food while singing hymns and speaking blessings and prayers, were expected to work permanently at their own inner schooling and transformation. They lived in accordance with the three vows they had made, and were therefore, because of their path of development, capable of transforming the food they took in. The *auditores*, the laity in the Manichaean community, meaning those who had not (yet) made the three vows, were not able to achieve this process of transformation. But by their presence at the ritual and their contribution to the gifts of the food, they participated in the purification and were also transformed.

Even more than in statements by Mani and in the scarce remains of Manichaean art, we see here the motif of the role of art in the context of Mani's view. In the end, the goal is to transform matter, earthly matter that, precisely because it consists in a mixture of light and darkness, carries this possibility in itself. The light that has connected itself with darkness, as a result of which matter could come into being, was called in Middle Persian *Griw Zindag*, the Living Soul, formed from the five light elements with which primal humanity girded itself before surrendering to be devoured by the powers of darkness. The powers of darkness thus scattered the light elements in innumerable fragments throughout the creation.

Yet, the ritual meal was not a memorial to the sacrifice of the pure Light Soul, later also called Jesus Patibilis. Neither was it a symbolic repetition of this deed. It is an event that takes place in the most physical part of the human being, the metabolism. And it is exactly here that the motif of art can become most evident. By the absorption of earthly substance and by the purification and transformation process that follows it, a newly born substance can "come to light." In a similar way, an artist can only by an intensely personal handling of the most earthly things contribute to a transfiguration of matter.

The Significance of the Picture

Ardahang is the usual Middle-Persian name of the Picture Book created by Mani. There is also another Middle Persian term, *negar-nama*, meaning illumination or illustration of a book. *Nigar* can also mean "painting" in the sense of any painted representation. Therefore, "picture" and "representation" are not identical concepts.

In this regard, Hans Joachim Klimheit spoke of an intuitive transfer of knowledge by means of the picture. "The picture is not a mere illustration; it is itself a manner of knowledge transfer."[60] There is, however, nothing left of Mani's Picture Book, so that we are unable to have an impression of the way it presented a path toward insight through the pictures. Neither is this possible through the miniature fragments that have been found, because these were made later by scribes and painters on the basis of what Mani had first accomplished.

At best we can draw a parallel between the picture as a path to insight into spiritual reality and the significance of the icon in the Byzantine world. In addition, the frequent use of pictures in language is characteristic for Manichaean scriptures. This is amply demonstrated in the preserved material. It is to Victoria Arnold-Doben's merit that she collected a number of these pictures used in language.[61] Many of these pictures, such as the "Light Cross" or the "Twins Call and Answer," speak for themselves, and they are striking by their power to bring things together in broad relationships. The fact that some pictures were used not only in language but also in painting proves their great importance in Mani's teaching.

A picture that has an important role is that of the tree. It has more than one significant aspect. Some of the meditation caves along the Silk Road have along both walls pictures of five flowering and five withered trees, as images of the soul elements of light and darkness. In the well-known cave of Bezeklik in the Turfan Oasis, there is a picture of a flowering jewel tree, flanked by six figures on each side, who worship the tree in their midst. The crown of the tree, which fills the entire wall, is carried by three trunks, each of which splits into two toward the top. The three trunks portray three epochs and the split into two indicates the two principles that go through three great time periods. The tree is decorated with lotus flowers and bunches of grapes formed from gemstones, always twelve in number. This "flowering jewel tree" was in the Manichaean tradition a picture of Mani himself, surrounded by twelve "light apostles" who worship him.

Rudolf Steiner on the Source of Art and Artistry

Rudolf Steiner did not mention Mani as an artist or the art impulse in Manichaeism. In 1913 an extensive report of the most important discoveries in Kucha in the Turfan Oasis appeared in Berlin, with many illustrations, including miniature fragments.[62] But the interest in this element of Manichaeism took a back seat behind the continuing attention that was rightfully given to the texts and that would still lead to important additional discoveries.

It seems as if the question of Mani as an artist, and the role of art in his teaching, is yet to receive consideration. For when it becomes evident that art not only has a prominent role in Manichaeism, but unites the revelation and preaching, the ritual and the community, into a living whole, then we come to the inescapable question of what the source of Mani's artistry is. What enables an individuality such as Mani, who called himself the Paraclete, also to be an artist?

In a lecture given in Vienna, [63] Rudolf Steiner spoke about the question of the connection between spiritual-scientific insight and being a creative artist: "The relationship between what one could call modern clairvoyance, as meant in anthroposophic Spiritual Science, and artistic creativity..." Artistic creativity and imaginative consciousness, as meant above, draw from one and the same source, although the way they express themselves is different. "The source, the true source from which the artist creates, is exactly the same as the source from which those who perceive the spiritual world gain their experiences." A little later he said, "But we may emphasize that the source from which the artist and the seer create is one and the same."

Applied to Mani, this would mean that his gazing into the spiritual world and his artistry would originate in the same source. In other words, Mani's artistry was not something incidental, something he was apparently also capable of, in the way it might be said of a highly gifted person that he was *also* an artist. What makes Mani unique is that he was able to unite these two aspects that, as Rudolf Steiner said, have one common origin, in his person. He was *seer* and *artist* in one. In the same lecture, Steiner explained how the one who has acquired insight into the reality of the spiritual also has the capacity of translating this insight into living concepts, while the artist incorporates this same insight in matter. Mani was known to translate his message into concepts that were current in whatever place he was preaching. Although this is often called "syncretism" one may also regard it as a form of art. After all, Mani incorporated his knowledge of spiritual reality, which had been inwardly revealed to him through his *syzygos*, into the "material" that was made available to him in a specific religious context. This knowledge was part of Mani as seer, while the ability to incorporate it in pre-existing "matter" was part of Mani as artist. In daily life, these two possibilities were, of course, always practiced together. This can also throw light on the statement we have quoted already: "My wisdom, I wrote it down in my scriptures, and I painted it in my pictures."

Both were part of his work with the goal of gradually pervading the Earth with purified light forces, so that at the end of time *Frashegird*, transfiguration, might take place.

Conclusion

Because in Mani the artist and the initiate were always working together, he is a unique figure amid the great wisdom teachers, prophets, and founders of religions. What he preached, and certainly the way he communicated his message, both were a form of art, just as the organization of his congregation showed the first beginning characteristics of a social architecture. Even louder than Mani's call to all human beings to lovingly discern in themselves the darkness and the light, we hear an invitation here to elevate the earthly in all facets of what it is to be human in such a way that it becomes able to realize its potential nature of light.

EPILOGUE: ANTHROPOSOPHY
AND MANICHAEISM AS DEED

"The aim of Manichaeism is to sublimate human beings to become redeemers." (CW 94)

Already in his first lecture about Manichaeism (CW 93), Rudolf Steiner put great emphasis on the aspect of this stream as preparation for a future "form of organization" and "founding of communities," in which it will be possible for Christian life to grow in this form, which has to be prepared ahead of time. He also spoke of a vessel: "[The Manichaeans] will provide an adequate vessel in the future." As mentioned before, he was very careful in these statements and avoided presenting concrete pictures of these "outer forms."

At other times, however, Steiner viewed the creation of new forms in which the life of a community can manifest itself as the ultimate goal of Anthroposophy. "True Anthroposophy must present as the final goal the community of free and independent "I"-beings that have become individualized. It is just this that is the mission of the Earth, which is expressed in love, that "I"-beings learn to confront one another freely" (CW 104).

In many respects, Rudolf Steiner put his life in service of this mission of the Earth, in order that as many people as possible would be able to have at their disposal the "instruments" they need for this. It depends on every human being individually to determine whether they want to engage in a similar willingness to serve. In a very explicit statement by Rudolf Steiner, the motif of the deed is clearly expressed: "If it [the Manichaean spiritual stream] were to function merely in the cultivation of an inner mood of soul, this current would not achieve what it should do" (CW 93).

If we want to collaborate in what Steiner described as the mission of the Earth, a task that points in the same direction as the Mani intention, then it does not suffice merely to cultivate the inner life. It can only be Mani intention if inner development is put in service of our fellow human being. And it is self-evident that we are not speaking only of like-minded individuals. The point is to serve every human being, no matter whom. For on the path of schooling, there is not one phase, not even the very highest, that can justify me to judge another person, and to know what would be good for him or her. We cannot make progress on this path if anything is done at the expense of "our brother."

No wisdom, no knowledge can help us if we do not actually "live this wisdom or knowledge." For it is out of this living that a new form will be born.

No matter to what extent the Mani intention points to the future, the inner gesture of the Manichaean impulse is also one of "looking back." It is the gesture of noticing the one who stays behind, rather than looking for the one who is already ahead on the path. Manichaeism is about concern for the brother or sister who is lagging behind.

> When you make a step forward in your development you cause the people who remain behind to find themselves in even deeper darkness than before. The path of the Manichaean is characterized by the practice that they fully devote themselves to their own development during a certain period of their lives. They then return to the poorest of the poor to share their lives with them.[64]

On this point Anthroposophy and the Manichaean stream can find each other, and Anthroposophy becomes a deed.

APPENDIX 1: MANU AND MANI

A question that to this day has not found a fully satisfactory answer is that of the relationship between Manu, the great Atlantean initiate, and Mani. First of all, their names seem to be similar. Among the many meanings of the Sanskrit verb-root *man* are *to think* and *spirit*, comparable to the many meanings of the Greek word *nous*, which also has to do with the human thinking capacity. *Manas* is a spiritual capacity of the human being that is often translated into English as *mind*. In Theosophy and Anthroposophy, *manas* means a higher capacity, namely the transformed astral body, and in this context it is translated as *spirit self*. In Indian Theosophy Manu (or the Manu) is a highly developed spiritual being that carries the leadership of the development of humanity with the purpose of initiating a new cultural period.

From Manichaean scriptures it appears that the name Mani (Manes in Greek and Latin) is of Aramaic origin. Aramaic is one of the Semitic languages and is related to Syriac. It was the language spoken by Jesus Christ. Mani is therefore a transcription of an originally Aramaic word that is usually written as *m'ny* and means *vessel*. The complete form of Mani's name is *m'anyxyws*, which means *the living Mani* and indicates Mani as the one who receives the Holy Spirit in himself as in a vessel—the embodiment of the Holy Spirit. It is a title, not a proper name.

A complete review of the various forms used for the name Mani in the original texts, together with references to the various authors who have written about this, can be found in www.iranicaonline.org/articles/mani-founder-Manicheism.

It becomes clear that we cannot conclude from the name, or rather the title, that there is indeed a relationship between Manu, the great initiate of the central Sun oracle of Atlantis, and Mani, the founder of Manichaeism.

Rudolf Steiner described in a number of lectures how Manu, before the destruction of Atlantis in the Great Flood, guided a small group of initiates to an area in Central Asia, now in the Gobi Desert, and that from there impulses were given for the subsequent cultures of which the Indian culture was the first one. Under the leadership of Manu the core of the wisdom that had been developed by the initiates of the Atlantean oracles was taken to a subsequent great phase of development.[65]

Rudolf Steiner also identified Manu with Noah: "Noah can be viewed as the leader Manu, who had to lead people out of Atlantis when it perished" (*Kosmogonie*, cw 94, July 6, 1906).

In his book *The Battle for the Soul* Bernard Lievegoed speaks of three great leaders of humanity and their mutual collaboration: Christian Rosenkreutz, Rudolf Steiner, and Manu. In regard to Manu, Lievegoed refers to a statement by Rudolf Steiner that the divine Manu will at some time become a human Manu. In Lievegoed's view, this transformation from the divine to the human Manu began in the Egyptian cultural epoch, and Mani would have been the third incarnation of the human Manu. The divine Manu belongs to the past of humanity; the era of the human Manu has begun and Mani was one of his incarnations. The task of the human Manu is to lead humanity on its path of fully absorbing the wisdom that was once developed in the oracles of Atlantis and make it an integral part of human inner life.

This ties in with Rudolf Steiner's lecture of August 31, 1909 (cw 113), in which he spoke of the change that the coming of Christ brought about on the Earth. From this time on, wisdom is no longer handed on from master to pupil as in the era of the divine Manu, but wisdom is transformed into brotherliness in the sign of the human Manu. However, at the end of this lecture, Rudolf Steiner spoke again about Mani, who called Skythianus, Buddha, and Zarathustra together into a suprasensory council, and he indicated that Mani is of a higher spiritual rank than the three teachers of humanity that he has assembled around himself.

Mani experienced himself as directly inspired by the Holy Spirit. Rudolf Steiner spoke in this regard of an "emanation."

Ehrenfried Pfeiffer (1899–1961), who knew Rudolf Steiner in the early 1920s, relates the following from a conversations with Steiner:

> We see that from now on Mani will be connected with the social order, with the question of a proper social order for human beings.... The threefold social order is particularly a preparatory work to bring about a future incarnation of Mani.... [Rudolf Steiner] said that Mani could not find a suitable body yet, that all the forces he would be able to bring to an incarnation would be destroyed by modern education. Therefore he said that the need was that the Waldorf School education be manifested and that the threefold social order be manifested.
>
> Therefore I would see it as our immediate task to bring about that threefold order, first through thought and then through action, so that Mani can incarnate. By karma, Mani's incarnation would be due by the end of the [twentieth] century. Whether this will be possible I do not know, but if the threefold social order and Waldorf education were established he could incarnate again.
>
> The followers of Mani who were incarnated as heretics in the twelfth to thirteenth centuries are to prepare for the end of this [the twentieth] century.[66]

APPENDIX 2:
THE MANICHAEAN VIEW
OF JESUS AND CHRIST

"Jesus, the 'I' in the 'Light-"I"' of all human beings..."

In a number of Gnostic systems during the first centuries after Christ, and in Manichaeism in particular, the idea of Christ's existence before he incarnated on the Earth was widely discussed. In Manichaeism, this idea was systematically developed. The pre-existent Christ descends to the Earth through several eons. In every eon a battle takes place with the powers of darkness, as a result of which the figure of Christ changes. In Manichaeism we encounter a developing Christ, until he enters into the earthly realm in the historical Jesus. In scientific circles there is a lively debate as to whether the Jesus Christ of the Manichaeans went through death on the cross (Adoptionism) or that he left the body before the death on the cross (Docetism).[67]

The Geography of Manichaeism

Manichaeism had its origin in the teaching that was proclaimed by Mani from approximately 240 CE in the then very large Persian Empire. Mani's life took place between the downfall of the dynasty of the Parthians and the new dynasty of the Sassanids. The Sassanids would, for the last time, bring to the empire peace and prosperity that lasted for centuries.

For a long time, the Persian Empire offered many different religions and sectarian movements, but during the last years of Mani's life it proclaimed Zarathustra's teaching (dating back to the sixth century BCE), now in the new form of Mazdaism, as the official state religion. Until then, Christianity, mostly in its Nestorian form, was widespread in Iran. But there were also countless Jewish-Christian communities, some of which strictly practiced purification by daily immersion in water. Besides Judaism there was Buddhism and even Hinduism. The ancient mysteries and cults had not yet altogether disappeared. The Mithras cult that traveled West with the Roman armies was of Iranian origin.

Mani's Life

Mani was born in 216 CE to the south of today's Baghdad. Mesopotamia at that time formed part of the Persian Empire. Not far from Baghdad lies Ctesiphon, the residence of both the Parthian and the later Sassanid rulers. Today there is still a remnant of the Iwan in Ctesiphon, a dome-shaped great hall in which the Persian King of Kings took part in official ceremonies, while behind him burned the holy fire and in front of him was pure water. In Zoroastrian tradition the earth elements were sacred, and the ruler represented the divine omnipotence that had created these elements that it was his duty to protect.

No doubt Mani's parents attended these festive ceremonies, at any rate until Mani's father had a divine inspiration to join a Baptist community that seems to have been founded by Elchasai. When Mani was four years old, his father took him away from his mother to bring him to this Baptist community. From this important event on it became clear that Mani had a divine task. Angel beings accompanied the child. One of these made himself known as Mani's *syzygos,* his spiritual image. Between his twelfth and twenty-fourth years Mani was initiated by this angel being in the mysteries of the heights and depths, in who he was, where he came from and what his mission was.

He would proclaim to all of humanity what was to be called a "good message," a gospel. It is the message of the origin of good and evil, and the role human beings have been given in this power play.

When Mani was twenty-four years old he left the community of Baptists in order to begin his mission. His father was one of his first followers. A life of incessant traveling and preaching, which would last thirty-five years, was then beginning. Mani went to the north of today's Iran, to Azerbaijan and the Caucasus. Then he turned to India following the footsteps of the Apostle Thomas. In the year 242 he was back at the court of King Shapur I and attended his coronation. He made a good impression on the King and the court, and received permission to preach publicly to large crowds of people. "He gave me permission to travel in his realm and to proclaim the word of life."[68]

Mani's Sentence and Death

However, the influence of Mazdaism remained great at the court. It came to the fore in the tension that grew between Mani and Bahram I (274–277), the second ruler after Shapur I. Mani was accused and had to appear at court. Kartir, the high priest of the magi (moghubed, the priests of Mazdaism), had the ear of Bahram I. He was Mani's actual opponent, and in memorial inscriptions on rocks that can still be read (for instance near Naqhs-e Rajab) he took pride in having persecuted and expelled the Manichaeans. In 276, Mani was executed in the city of Gondishapur (Syrian beth Lapat), now a ruin close to Dezful in southwestern Iran. In documents discovered among other places in Egypt, Mani's last conversations with the companions that surrounded him to the end have been preserved. Mani expressed his longing to be allowed to return to the light realm of "His Father," but now freed from his earthly fetters. Mani's passion, which lasted almost a month, and his death formed the subject of the most important liturgical festival of the Manichaeans: a month of fasting ending in the great Bema festival preceded by a night-long wake, until with the first sunlight Mani was spiritually present in the midst of the community.

Despite persistent persecution, Mani's teaching was able to spread from west to east. For the longest time there were Manichaean communities along the northern branch of the Silk Road, now in north-west China. In the eighth century, the Uighur rulers who had recently settled there adopted Manichaeism. Mani had himself documented his teaching in seven great books. The eighth work is a picture book in which he himself had painted his cosmogony. Mani put great emphasis on the fact that he had himself written down his wisdom and expressed it in pictures. Copying the sacred texts in beautiful calligraphy, and illustrating them with miniatures, was an essential part of life in a Manichaean community.

Due to the amazing discoveries made in the twentieth century, it has become possible to have access to original Manichaean scriptures, while until that time we were limited to documents from quite unreliable opponents such as Church Fathers, or more reliable but not always well-informed Arabic historians.

Scriptures

Mani usually wrote in Aramaic, a kind of *lingua franca* in the Middle East at the time. An exception is the Shabuhragan, which Mani wrote in Middle Persian at the request of King Shapur I. Then there is the *Living Gospel*, divided into twenty-two chapters for the twenty-two letters in the Syriac alphabet. This has important biographical elements and can be viewed as the most important of Mani's scriptures. Other scriptures are the *Book of Giants*, the so-called *Pragmateia* (very little of which is known), and the *Book of Mysteries*. Almost nothing was preserved of these books except what was written by Christian polemicists. There are also many sermons by Mani that were collected in the so-called *Kephalaia*, as well as letters, homilies, psalms, and prayers. Most of these have been preserved in Coptic. Finally there is the *Picture Book* that was mentioned already.

The various discoveries of original Manichaean documents can be divided into two great groups:

1. A first group of findings was made along the Silk Road near the oasis of Turfan, now in north-west China, by successive expeditions from 1902 to 1904. The totality of these documents gives access to what can be called by the general name of *Iranian Manichaica*. The reference to Iran here is not to the language but to the general cultural situation.

2. From 1930, a second group of scriptures was found in Egypt. These discoveries should be seen against the background of the early development of Coptic Christianity in these areas. These documents were written in Coptic and are generally referred to as the *Coptic Manichaica*.

We have to make special mention of the pictures: several dozens of miniature fragments that were all found along the Silk Road, most of which are now in the Museum for Indian Art in Berlin.

Finally, in a remarkable discovery in 1969, a codex was found in Egypt that was purchased by the University of Cologne and formed part of a larger codex, the so-called Cologne Mani Codex (CMC). By its format alone already this little book is unique: not much larger than a postage stamp, it consists of 190 pages written in Greek. It contains a kind of autobiography of Mani from his fourth year to the time of his first public appearance. The rest, which described the continuation of his life, was lost.

In the Cologne Mani Codex Mani's *syzygos* calls him to his mission:

> You were not sent to this religion only [the Elchasaites] but to all peoples, all schools, every city and every place; for

through you this hope will be declared and proclaimed in all zones and places of the world. In very great numbers people will accept your word. Act therefore in public and look round; for I shall be with you as your helper and protector in every place if you proclaim everything I have revealed to you. Therefore, have no care and be not sad.[69]

Manichaeism and Gnostic Streams

Manichaeism appeared in a world in which Gnosticism still had great influence. It had also spread into existing religions and worship services. It is not possible to form a true and profound conception of Manichaeism without considering it against the background of these Gnostic streams. In spite of the great variety of Gnostic streams, it is possible to recognize some general characteristics.

The Greek word *gnosis* means "knowledge," but not knowledge that can be added to a store of already acquired knowledge, such as information that can be saved in the brain as on a storage disk. Gnosis is knowledge by experience. It consists of an insight that, at the moment a person reaches the insight, radically changes him or her, and as a result of which every further experience leads to insight, and the other way around.

Gnosis has to do with the great mysteries of life. The origin of humankind had to be understood from the totality of Gnostic cosmogony. That cosmogony described how, in the original light world, a crisis took place because one of the light beings separated from the whole. This act, which was later reversed, led to a catastrophe. A dark abyss opened that was none other than the world of creation itself. This creation, which had not been intended or willed by the divine light world, could not be undone.

Eventually the human being was created who, by the intervention of the light beings, was endowed with a divine spark. Insight then meant lighting this spark. Once one was awakened, it was inevitable that this awareness led to the insight that one could only return to the light world on condition that one did not become connected with the world of darkness of matter. Physical-material existence itself was evil, while the light world made an exclusive claim on the good. Human beings who had arrived at insight had to take their destiny in their own hands. They were exiles in the created world; they did not belong there. They could find their way back to their true home, provided that they turned radically away from everything that belonged to the created world. They had to arm themselves against this world and, if necessary, fight it in order to bring about their own redemption.

It is really questionable whether Manichaeism also taught such an absolute dualism. An essential distinction, often overlooked, is the fact that the Manichaeism cosmogony begins with two principles: the principle of Light and the principle of Darkness, which at a certain stage become mingled with each other and both participate in the act of creation. By contrast, the cosmogony of Gnosticism starts out with one single principle, the Light.

The consequence of this crucial difference is that in Manichaeism the creation was a matter of light *and* darkness, while in Gnosticism we hear of a catastrophe and an unplanned event in which the light was hurled into its opposite, darkness, and came down into the creation. Unlike in Manichaeism, the created world was then equated completely with the Realm of Darkness.

The Five Manifestations of the Redeemer

It is not possible to interpret the different manifestations of Jesus and Christ in Manichaeism without going into the teaching more deeply. Manichaeism shares with Gnostic streams the fact that it is a doctrine of salvation. Humanity is in a situation in which its continued existence is threatened, so that help and redemption have become necessary. This indicates the perspective from which the repeated intervention by Jesus and the appearance of Christ have to be understood. It also looks as if we have to make a distinction between Jesus (in Aramaic called *Isa*) and Christ (indicated with the word *Masyah*, the anointed one). But it turns out that it is not possible to be consistent in this distinction; in Manichaeism itself it is also not consistently maintained.

We will therefore describe five manifestations, although we know that in doing so we have not exhausted the subject. In addition, Manichaeism shares with the Gnostic systems the teaching that the essence of the human being can be fully understood only through a cosmogony. The cosmogony leads to anthropology—these are inseparable from each other. For this reason we will first shed light on these two aspects of Mani's teaching so that we will be able to place the manifestations of Jesus and Christ in their context.

The Cosmogony of Mani

Among the discoveries along the Silk Road a treatise in Chinese was found in which the teaching of Mani is represented as the doctrine of the two principles and the three eras. The two primal creative principles are darkness and light. They have existed since the primeval beginning of time, even before creation.

In the first era the two principles stand side by side and are in a state of deep rest. Each principle is focused on itself, on maintaining its own nature, and has no knowledge of the existence of the other. They are occupied within themselves. The light realm borders to the south on the realm of darkness, but the two realms are completely separate: a state of absolute dualism.

The second era begins when the realm of darkness catches a glimpse of the light realm. This causes great agitation and the beings of the realm of darkness prepare to invade the light realm, so that they can take the light for themselves.

This critical situation is noticed by the light realm, where-upon the Father of Light (the Father of Greatness) decides to meet the darkness. He emanates out of himself the Mother of Life, who in her turn calls into existence the first human being, the as yet uncreated Adam Cadmon, who will now face the massing multitude of the darkness. First he girds himself with five pure light elements that together form his light soul. An important factor is that the light realm does not resist the attack of the realm of darkness; it remains true to its own light nature, which is mildness and peacefulness. Any gesture of defense or counterattack would have made a change in this light nature.

The first human being is seized by the powers of darkness and cries for help. The Living Spirit descends from the light world to save him, but he loses his light soul, which is torn to pieces and finally devoured by the powers of darkness. In the end, a new substance comes into being: a mixed substance resulting from the complete mingling of light and darkness. The state of absolute dualism thus develops into a dynamic dualism.

In order not to leave the light soul to its own devices, a creative process is begun. The creation is brought into existence from the mixed substance; the powers of darkness and light participate alternately in this event of creation. At this time, the first human being, Adam, is in a state of deep sleep. The question now is how he can gain consciousness, or gnosis. But the creation is complete, meaning that any further development is in human hands.

The cosmogony now transitions to anthropology. The question of how the creation came to be has been answered. The next question is this: To what purpose has the human being appeared in the creation? This purpose, the finality of the event of creation, is contained in its origin. Nevertheless, the central focus has shifted from a cosmic battlefield to the human being.

The Human Being

"Learn to discern! Put on your crown of light!" With these words, Jesus the Splendor awakens Adam's consciousness from its sleep. The discernment is a distinction between what in our own nature comes from the light and what comes from the darkness. This discernment is at the same time the first beginning of a work of redemption.

By the sacrifice of the Light Father, which was continued by the first human being, a new substance comes into being from which the creation is formed. The central point in this creation is the human being, a being of light and darkness. By entering on a path of insight in regard to our own nature, which we can learn to understand from its origin, we take a central position in the work of redemption. The future wellbeing of creation is in our hands. Learning to know our own nature reveals to us at the same time the purpose of our existence: by using the forces of good to begin liberating the forces of evil from their compelling nature, we eventually redeem everything in creation that is still fettered in the forces of darkness. The third era cannot become a real possibility until human beings take this process in hand.

The mingling of light and darkness makes the third era possible, for in and from the darkness the light can now work and shine in the darkness. This light shining in the darkness leads to the third era, when a new Earth and a new cosmos come into being. The Earth will be transformed into a light Earth, a new creation in which the light has transfigured the darkness. This is not a return to an original condition, but the eventual result of the further development of the creation to a new cosmos of wisdom and love in which human beings fulfill a decisive role.

And the old Earth, the dwelling place of the enemies, the house of darkness, has been overthrown and annihilated.

And on it we, the Gods of the Light, have built the shining foundation of the New Aeon.[70]

Thus we see that in Manichaeism we can speak of a radical dualism only in the first era. With the events in the second and third eras we encounter the interaction of light and darkness that results in the creation as well as the potential of redemption. It would be correct to speak here of a dynamic dualism that changes its radicalism in the course of a process of transformation.

Christ and Jesus

Manichaeism speaks of more than one manifestation of Christ and of Jesus. One way of making a certain distinction in the sometimes-confusing use of these two names is by taking into account that in many respects Jesus is viewed as a missionary, a helper, a messenger from the light realm. This role may be compared with that of a prophet. Prophets are messengers who communicate a particular revelation to humanity. More than once, Mani placed himself in the line of prophets that had preceded him. Jesus is one of them, but in the figure of a prophet who brings revelations from the divine world.

The name Christ indicates an identity of being with the light realm. It is striking that in this connection Mani points to himself as having been sent by Jesus Christ. In the hymns— in which the soul expresses its longing for the light realm— Christ is often invoked. By contrast, Jesus is the one who assists the human beings on Earth in their struggle to fathom their own nature. The words that Jesus the Splendor directs to Adam, who comes to himself and becomes aware of his situation on Earth, are full of compassion, but are also strict. Adam must take his own salvation and that of the rest of creation into his own hands. Jesus did not come to save him, but to provide him with the instruments he needs for his redemption. The response lies in Adam himself.

The Different Manifestations

1. Jesus Christ as Cosmic Principle

The Father of Greatness, or King of the Light Realm, can be understood as the being who holds together and carries in himself the whole of the light world. The moment the light becomes active and reveals itself, this changes. At that moment, Christ is the one through whom the light nature of the Father is revealed. Each time a light revelation of the Light Father is mentioned, we are witnessing a manifestation of Christ.

In this same manifestation Christ fulfills a role when in a certain phase of the creative process he takes his place as "Light Revelation" in the spiritual spheres of sun and moon. There also originates the impulse that accompanies the darkness through these spheres when it has been liberated and purified to light.

It is important that these several manifestations of Christ do not penetrate into the sphere of the Earth, but they dwell and act in the (cosmic) realms where a redemption of the darkness is already taking place. A second important aspect of this macrocosmic Christ is that he is the light side of the Father of Greatness turned outward. Both aspects operate in the so-called second condition, in which light and darkness penetrate into each other so that out of that state the work of redemption can be begun.

A third aspect, which is related to this, is that of Christ as the Column of Glory, or the "Last Stature." The purified darkness—in other words, transformed matter—"grows" as a vertical column of light in the center of creation, and stretches between the light realm and the Earth. When the Earth will have been fully transformed, the third condition will have been achieved. Transformed matter, a completely new substance, finally becomes the new body of Christ:

He carries upward...until the last hour, when he shall awaken and place himself in the great fire and collect his own soul in himself and form himself to the "Last Stature"; and you shall find him, how he rises up and casts off the impurity, which is foreign to him; the life, however, and the light that is in all things he collects in himself and he builds his body thereof .[71]

2. *Jesus Patibilis*

Jesus Patibilis coincides completely with the light soul of the first human being. This light soul is formed from the five pure light elements, also called the sons of the primal human being. Once it has been seized by the powers of darkness this soul is torn into countless little light particles and imprisoned in the darkness. These light elements form the life principle for the beings of the different kingdoms of nature: mineral, plant, and animal, beings that are not capable of insight, and therefore redemption, and that consequently have to suffer. More accurately: the light soul suffers in each of them. The totality of this light soul, which exists in countless fragments throughout the creation, forms the figure of Jesus Patibilis.

A different picture, which expresses the same situation, is that of the light cross that is part of the earthly creation and embraces the world soul in its four arms.

The manifestation of Jesus Patibilis must be strictly distinguished from that in which Jesus acts as helper of humanity. Here we are speaking of the light soul that is imprisoned in the creatures of nature and that cries to be liberated. The helper here is the human being who possesses the potential of insight and therefore redemption:

Endow me with a sacred heart, my God; make new in me a sincere spirit. The sacred heart is Christ; if he rises in us, we rise in him. Christ is risen; we shall rise with him. If we believe in him, we shall go beyond death and come to life.[72]

3. Jesus as Judge

This manifestation of Jesus occurs when the third condition begins, when good and evil can interact for the last time. Jesus will then act as World Judge. The evil that cannot be redeemed will contract into a sphere and will be hurled into the cosmos. This may sound surprising. However, it may also be understood as creating the potential for a new cycle, in which again good and evil, interacting with each other but now at a higher level, make a contribution to the plan of creation.

4. Jesus the Splendor

Jesus the Splendor has the important role of assisting the human being on Earth. He stands precisely there where cosmogony changes into anthropology. Jesus calls Adam by his name, and thus calls him to himself. Now Adam receives instruction so that he can learn to distinguish between good and evil of his own accord. This enables the Light *Nous*, the principle of independence, the spiritual element, to become active in him. From this development it becomes clear that Jesus the Splendor is at the same time equated with the Light *Nous*. For in this role, Jesus can awaken the Light *Nous* in the human being because he himself represents this element.

Here we can also trace the development of one Jesus manifestation to the following one. Jesus Patibilis unites the five light elements of the light soul, which are unfree and are condemned to suffering in their imprisonment in nature. Jesus the Splendor represents the principle that can lead to liberation. As a result, the five light elements (light, water, earth, fire, and air) are eventually transformed into five spiritual capacities, namely discernment, insight, thinking, contemplation, and consciousness. Together, these five are called the perfect human being, the New Adam, who brings himself into being through the process of transformation within creation.

5. The Historical Jesus

Manichaeism also speaks of the earthly life and death of Jesus of Nazareth. In often moving words his passion is described as a model of the way in which the greatest purity is sacrificed in the dynamic between good and evil. An important point is therefore how this sacrifice may be understood. In many Gnostic streams the death on the cross of Jesus of Nazareth was described as a semblance, since this divine being had sojourned on Earth in the semblance of a body (Docetism).

Some passages in texts that were recently translated (*Chinese Hymn*, Alberry Collection, London) show, however, that in Manichaeism the death on the cross is viewed in such a way that the sacrifice of Jesus can be interpreted as a pure sacrifice of love. He sacrifices his divine omnipotence so that he can become mortal like a human being. Out of boundless compassion the divine adopts the human condition in the human Jesus, and unites itself with him:

> From the coming of Zarathustra until the coming of Jesus Christ, the Son of Greatness. The coming of Jesus Christ, our Lord. He came... in the spiritual, in a body as I [Mani] have spoken about Him.... He came without body. On their part the Apostles proclaimed of Him that He adopted the form of a servant, an appearance as of a human being. He descended and revealed Himself in the sect of the Jews.... Satan entered into Judas Iscariot, one of the twelve of Jesus. He accused Jesus with the sect of the Jews, by his kiss he gave Him into the hands of the Jews and the cohorts of soldiers. The Jews... nailed him to the cross, they crucified Him together with robbers. They took Him down again from the cross and laid Him in the grave, and after three days He rose from the dead and came to His disciples and appeared to them.[73]

We note that in other passages, however, it looks much more as if a kind of Docetic view was living also in Manichaeism.

Conclusion

From the foregoing we can see how deeply Manichaeism is connected with Christianity. For this reason, it is right to understand Manichaeism as a continuation and deepening of Christianity in its earliest form, in which the manifestations of Jesus and Christ, in spite of the different ways in which they can be interpreted, have a decisive role.

On the other hand, much of what lives in these manifestations is still just a seed. It asks for a continuation, in the direction of a condition in which the countenance of Jesus and the countenance of Christ become one single countenance, in which all human beings recognize themselves.

NOTES

1   J. van Schaik, *Gnostiek en Antroposofie*, Christofoor, Zeist, 2010.

2   B. Lievegoed, *The Battle for the Soul* (the original Dutch title translates as "On the Salvation of the Soul"), Hawthorn Press, 1994.

3   Ibid.

4   P. Mirecki and J. BeDuhn, *Emerging from Darkness: Studies in the Recovery of Manichaean Sources*, Brill, 1997.

5   Isaac de Bausobre, *Histoire critique de Man et de Manichée*, Amsterdam, 1734.

6   G. Haloun and W. B. Henning, in *Asia Minor, New Series*, vol. 3, part 2, London, 1952.

7   Chavannes-Pelliot, "Un traité manichéen retrouvé en Chine," in *Journal Asiatique*, 1913.

8   C. G. Schmidt and H. J. Polotsky, *Ein Mani-Fund in Aegypten*, SPAW, Berlin, 1933.

9   A. Henrichs and L. Koenen, *Ein griechischer Mani Codex*, 1970 and ed. *Der Koelner Mani Kodex* (P. Colon, Inv. No. 4780), 1975–1982.

10   Translated into French and annotated by Nahal Tajadod, *Mani, le Bouddha de Lumière, Catechisme manichéen chinois*, Paris, 1990.

11   *Cologne Mani Codex*, translated by Ron Cameron and Arthur J. Dewey, Society of Biblical Literature 1979.

12   Rudolf Steiner, *Building Stones for an Understanding of the Mystery of Golgotha*, CW 175, Rudolf Steiner Press 1972, Apr. 19, 1917.

13   Rudolf Steiner, *The Temple Legend*, CW 93, Rudolf Steiner Press, 1985, Nov. 11, 1904.

14 Rudolf Steiner, *At the Gates of Spiritual Science*, CW 95, Rudolf Steiner Press, 1976, Aug. 29, 1906.

15 Rudolf Steiner, *The Apocalypse of St. John*, CW 104, Rudolf Steiner Press, 1985, June 25, 1908.

16 Rudolf Steiner, *An Esoteric Cosmology*, CW 94, SteinerBooks, 2008, chap. 2.

17 CW 93.

18 Rudolf Steiner, *The Philosophy of Thomas Aquinas*, CW 74, May 22, 1920.

19 J. van Oort, *Augustinus und der Manichaeismus* in: *The Manichaean Nous*, Manichaean Studies II, Lovanii 1995.

20 F. Decret, "Le dogme manichéen fondamental des deux principes selon Faustus de Milev," in *Manichaean Studies I: Manichaica Selecta*, Lovan.

21 I. Gardner and S. Lieu, *Manichaean Texts from the Roman Empire*, Cambridge, 2004.

22 See John van Schaik, *Antroposofie en geesteswetenschap*, Christofoor, 2010.

23 CW 94.

24 Rudolf Steiner, *Okkultes Lesen und okkultes Hören*, CW 156, Dec. 26, 1914.

25 Rudolf Steiner, *How Can Mankind Find the Christ Again?*, CW 187, Anthroposophic Press, 1984, December 25, 1918.

26 CW 93, introduction to the endnotes to the lecture of Nov. 11, 1904.

27 Rudolf Steiner, *The Mysteries of the East and of Christianity*, CW 144, Rudolf Steiner Press, 1972, Feb. 4, 1913.

28 See also *Alexander of Lycopolis on the Manichaean System* in: I. Gerdner & S. Lieu, *Manichaean Texts from the Roman Empire*, Cambridge 2004.

29 Andrea Piras, "Alessandro di Licopoli contro le Dottrine di Mani," in *Il Manichaeismo*, vol. 2: *Il Mito e la Dottrina, I testi Manichei Copti e la Polemica Antimanichea, a cura di Gherardo Gnoli*, 2006.

30 R. Contini, "Mani e il Manic heismo nella tradizione Syriaca," in *Il Manichaeismo*, vol. 2, 2006

31 W. Sundermann, *Cosmogony and Cosmology* in: *Manichaeism*, Rome, 2001.

32 J. van Oort, *Würdigung Isaac de Beausobres, Studia Manichaica*, IV, Internationaler Kongress zum Manichaeismus, Berlin, 2000.

33 For more detail see Julien Ries, *Introduction aux Etudes Manichéennes*.

34 G. Flügel, *Mani, seine Lehre und seine Schriften*, Leipzig, 1862

35 K. Kessler, *Mani, Forschungen über die manichäische Religion*, Berlin, 1889.

36 Th. Haarbrücken, Abu'-l-Fath, *Muhammed asch-Scharastani's Religionsparteien und Philosophenschulen*, 2 vol., Halle, 1850–1851.

37 A. von Harnack, "Der Manichaeismus," in *Lehrbuch der Dogmengeschichte*, Freiburg, 1886.

38 J. van Schaik, *Unde malum? Dualisme bij Manicheers en Katharen*, Ten Have 2004.

39 Rudolf Steiner, *The Need for Understanding the Christ*, CW 224, Apr. 29, 1923.

40 Rudolf Steiner, *Die Naturwissenschaft und die weltgeschichtliche Entwickelung der Menschheit seit dem Altertum*, CW 325, May 15, 1921.

41 Rudolf Steiner, *Das Zusammenwirken des Menschen mit der elementarischen Welt*, CW 158, Nov. 22, 1914.

42 Rudolf Steiner, *The Philosophy of Freedom*, CW 4, Anthroposophic Press, 1964, chap. 2.

43 Ibid., chap. 4.

44 CW 104.

45 H.-Ch. Puech, *Le manichéisme, son fondateur, sa doctrine*, Paris, 1949.

46 M 5794 in Mary Boyce, *A Reader in Manichaean Middle Persian and Parthian*, Leiden-Liege, 1975, *Acta Iranica*, 9, 29.

47 Notes in the chapter "From the Teachings about the Masters of Wisdom and of the Harmony of Sensations and Feelings" in Rudolf Steiner, *From the History and Contents of the First Section of the Esoteric School 1904–1914*, CW 264, Anthroposophic Press, 1998.

48 Rudolf Steiner, *The Gospel of St. Luke*, CW 114, Rudolf Steiner Press, 1964, Sept. 26, 1909.

49 CW 264, comment recorded by Ehrenfried Pfeiffer from his conversations with Rudolf Steiner between 1919 and 1921.

50 Rudolf Steiner, *The East in the Light of the West*, CW 113, Cornerstone Book Publishers 2011.

51 Rudolf Steiner, *From Symptom to Reality in Modern History*, CW 185, Rudolf Steiner Press ,1976, Oct. 26, 1918.

52 Rudolf Steiner, *Evolution in the Aspect of Realities*, CW 132, Garber, 1989.

53 CW 93.

54 B Lievegoed, op. cit., note 2.

55 CW 185.

56 M. Heuser and H.-J. Klimheit, *Studies in Manichaean Literature and Art*, Brill, 1998.

57 H.-J. Klimheit, *The Nature of Manichaean Art*, in M. Heuser and H.-J. Klimheit, *Studies in Manichaean Literature and Art*, Brill, 1998.

58 Z. Gulaczi, *Manichaean Art in Berlin Collections*, Brepols and Publishers.

59 H.-J. Klimheit, *Manichaeische Kunst an der Seidenstrasse, Alte und Neue Funde*, Nordrhein-Westphalische Akademie der Wissenschaften, Vortrage G 338, Westdeutsche Verlag.

60 Ibid.

61 Victoria Arnold-Doben, *Die Bildersprache des Manichäismus*, Kommission bei E. J. Brill, Cologne, 1978

62 Albert von le Coq, *Chotscho, Ergebnisse der Kgl. Preussischen Turfan Expeditionen*, Berlin, 1913.

63 Rudolf Steiner, *Kunst und Kunst Erkenntnis*, CW 271, June 1, 1918.

64 B. Lievegoed, op. cit.

65 Rudolf Steiner, *The Christian Mystery*, CW 97, Completion Press, 2000, Mar. 7, 1907.

66 E. Pfeiffer, *Notes and Lectures; Compendium I*, Mercury Press, 1991, Dec. 22, 1946.

67 This chapter first appeared in: John van Schaik (Ed.), *Het Beeld van Jezus Christus (The Image of Jesus Christ)*, Zeist, 2002.

68 *Kephalaia* I, 15–29, tr. I. Gardner, *The Kephalaia of the Teacher: The Edited Coptic Manichaean Texts in Translation with Commentary*, Leiden/New York/Cologne, 1995.

69 *Cologne Mani Codex* 104–5, *Koelner Mani Codex*, ed. L. Koenen and C. Roemer (tr. from Dutch P.M.).

70 *Shabuhragan* in: M. Boyce, *A Reader in Manichaean Middle Persian and Parthian*, Leiden, 1974 (tr. from Dutch P.M.).

71 *Kephalaia*, XVI, 54, 12–19 (tr. from Dutch P.M.).

72 *Book of Psalms*, 159 (tr. from Dutch P.M.).

73 *Kaphalaia*, I, 12: 19–35, 13:1–8 (tr. from Dutch P.M.).

BIBLIOGRAPHY

Baur, F. C. *Das Manichaeische Religionssystem nach den Quellen neu untersucht und entwickelt*, 1831.

de Beausobre, Isaac. *Histoire critique de Manichée et du Manichéisme*, 1734.

von Döllinger, Ignaz. *Beiträge zur Sektengeschichte des Mittelalters. 1. Geschichte der gnostisch-Manichaeischen Sekten*, Munich, 1890.

Colditz, F. E. *Die Entstehung des manichaeischen Religionssystems historisch-kritisch untersucht*, Leipzig, 1837.

Flügel, G. *Mani, seine Lehre und seine Schriften, Ein Beitrag zur Geschichte des Manichaeismus. Aus dem Fihrist des Ibn al-Nadim*, Leipzig, 1862.

von Harnack, A. *Der Manichaeismus,ein Lehrbuch der Dogmengeschichte*, Freiburg, 1886.

Heuser, M. and H.-J. Klimheit, *Studies in Manichaean Literature and Art*, Leiden-Boston-Cologne, 1998.

Kessler, K. *Untersuchungen zur Genesis des Manichaeischen Religionssytem*, Leipzig, 1875.

———, *Mani, Forschungen über die Manichaeische Religion*, Berlin, 1889.

Lievegoed, B. *The Battle for the Soul*, Stroud, UK: Hawthorn Press, 1994.

Reitzenstein, R. *Das iranische Erlösungsmysterium, Religionsgeschichtliche Untersuchungen*, Bonn, 1921.

Seddon, R. *Mani, His Life and Work: Transforming Evil*, London: Rudolf Steiner Press, 1998.

van Vliet, R. *Manichaeismus—das Christentum von Freiheit und Liebe*, Verlag Urachhaus, 2013.

Welburn, A. *Mani: the Angel and the Column of Glory, An Anthology of Manichaean Texts*, Edinburgh: Floris Books, 1998.

LECTURES BY RUDOLF STEINER

CW 74, May 22, 1920 (*The Redemption of Thinking: A Study in the Philosophy of Thomas Aquinas.* Hudson, NY: Anthroposophic Press, 1983).

CW 93, November 11, 1904 (*The Temple Legend: Freemasonry and Related Occult Movements.* London: Rudolf Steiner Press, 1997).

CW 94, May 16, 1906 (*An Esoteric Cosmology: Evolution, Christ & Modern Spirituality.* Great Barrington, MA: SteinerBooks, 2008).

CW 95, August 29, 1906 (*Founding a Science of the Spirit.* London: Rudolf Steiner Press, 1999).

CW 104, June 25, 1908 (*The Apocalypse of St. John: Lectures on the Book of Revelation.* Hudson, NY: Anthroposophic Press, 1985).

CW 113, August 31, 1909 (*The East in the Light of the West/Children of Lucifer.* Blauvelt, NY: Garber, 1986).

CW 156, December 26, 1914 (*Inner Reading and Inner Hearing: And How to Achieve Existence in the World of Ideas.* Great Barrington, MA: SteinerBooks, 2008).

CW 158, November 22, 1914 (*Der Zusammenhang des Menschen mit der elementarischen Welt;* not available in English).

CW 175, April 19, 1917 (*Building Stones for an Understanding of the Mystery of Golgotha.* London, Rudolf Steiner Press, 1972).

CW 187, December 25, 1918 (*Death as Metamorphosis of Life: Including "What Does the Angel Do in our Astral Body?" & "How Do I Find Christ?"* Great Barrington, MA: SteinerBooks, 2008).

CW 224, April 29, 1923 (*Die menschliche Seele in ihrem Zusammenhang mit göttlich-geistigen Individualitäten;* not available in English).

CW 325, May 15, 1921 (*Die Naturwissenschaft und die weltgeschichtliche Entwickelung der Menschheit seit dem Altertum;* not available in English).

CPSIA information can be obtained at www.ICGtesting.com
Printed in the USA
BVOW04s1830300914

368856BV00002B/3/P